TO CHERISH ALL LIFE

TO CHERISH ALL LIFE

A Buddhist View of
Animal Slaughter
and
Meat Eating

ROSHI PHILIP KAPLEAU

The Zen Center
Rochester, New York
1981

OTHER BOOKS BY PHILIP KAPLEAU

The Three Pillars of Zen
(revised and expanded)

The Wheel of Death

Zen: Dawn in the West

ISBN: 0-940306-00-X

Library of Congress Catalog # 81-51149

To Elsie, Porky, and Donald

TABLE OF CONTENTS

ACKNOWLEDGMENTS

I salute with deep gratitude the following people, without whose assistance this book would not have been possible: Bodhin Shakya, who researched and wrote supplements 1, 2, and 3 and helped me in many other important ways; Richard Wehrman who gave freely of his time and skills in designing the book and cover; Deborah Flynn who tirelessly attended to the exacting details of the mechanics of the design process and in addition photographed the animal sculptures for the illustrations; Marcy Apfelbaum and Jay Stratton who undertook the difficult task of typesetting; and Polly Papageorge who was a conscientious typist and secretary.

My special thanks to Professor Peter Singer for his permission to quote freely from his acclaimed book *Animal Liberation*, and to Richard Ellis for allowing me to reproduce his whale painting from the book *Vanishing Giants—the History, Biology and Fate of the Great Whales*.

INTRODUCTION

If, as the Genesis story tells us, man first sinned when Adam ate the apple Eve tempted him with in the Garden of Eden, surely his second great sin was succumbing to the temptation to kill and eat his fellow creatures, an event that may have first taken place during one of the glacial periods in prehistoric times when plant life, man's original diet, temporarily disappeared under sheets of ice, or it may have happened because of the pride and prestige associated with the killing of the huge mammals that dominated large portions of the earth when man the hunter came upon the scene. In any case, terror, violence, bloodshed, the slaughter of men, and ultimately war, it can be argued, all grew out of that fateful encounter.

Today there are few corners of the world where a hostile environment compels man to slaughter his four-legged kin, in imitation of his flesh eating ancestors, in order to sustain himself. On the contrary, plant food in all its richness and variety is abundantly available in most areas of the world. Yet the subjugation of the animal kingdom and the senseless war of aggression against it continues unabated. And a relentlessly cruel war it is, nowhere more so than on the farm, in the stockyards, and in the slaughterhouses. This is especially true today when the business of raising and slaughtering livestock for food in the developed countries has been largely taken over by multinational corporations. The first section of this book, which factually describes the frustration, pain, and terror suffered by animals destined for dinner tables, is intended to acquaint readers with these sufferings so they may better understand the rationale of the precept of not to kill but to preserve life.

Almost as frightful as the cruelties inflicted on livestock is the maltreatment of animals utilized for experimental research in the laboratories of universities, the military establishments of developed countries, and large commercial enterprises. Although this aspect of the oppression of animals is outside the scope of this treatise, it is nevertheless worth touching upon. Millions of primates, dogs, cats, sheep, rabbits, pigs, birds, rodents, and other animals are routinely subjected to experiments and tests that can be described at best as a torment and at worst as agonizingly lethal to them. It is estimated that nearly 70 million animals were "sacrificed" to research in 1980 alone. The usual justification for this testing is that it is indispensable to gaining vital knowledge that cannot be gotten otherwise than by utilizing human beings in the experiments, and that if it were prohibited it would seriously interfere with research that ultimately benefits humanity. Many scientists disagree with these contentions. One scientist, Dr. Bennett Derby, an eminent neurologist, is authority for the statement that 90 percent of animal experiments are repetitive and inadequate.[1] Other researchers say that a great deal of testing yields only trivial results, that much is unreliable because of interspecies inapplicability, and that in many cases the information sought can be more humanely and more advantageously obtained through *in vitro* testing and other non-animal alternatives now available but little utilized. In fact so alarmed have a number of scientists become about the dimensions of pointless animal testing that they have formed an organization, the Scientists' Center for Animal Welfare, to protect experimental animals from the cruel excesses of their unfeeling colleagues.

No discussion of animal welfare would be meaningful that did not deal with the morality of flesh eating. Since I have chosen to put this subject in the context of Buddhism, it seemed desirable, first of all, to discuss the significance of the first precept in Buddhism of not to take life. This in turn raises two fundamental questions: Can the first precept be fairly construed to prohibit meat eating? and second, Is there reliable evidence that the Buddha sanctioned flesh eating? A further question, bearing on the first two, is this: Did the Buddha die of eating a piece of pork, as claimed by some scholars, or from a poisonous mushroom, as asserted by others? If the statements of the *Pali*[2] texts, which presume to be a record of the Buddha's words, are accepted at face value, it can be argued that the Buddha allowed the eating of animal flesh in all cases except when one has reason to believe the animal one is about to eat was slaughtered expressly for one's dinner. This view, however, is flatly contradicted by the *Mahayana*[3] sutras, also purporting to be the spoken words of the Buddha, which categorically assert that flesh eating is contrary to the spirit and intent of the first precept since it makes one an accessory to the slaying of animals and therefore contravenes the compassionate concern for all life that lies at the core of Buddhism.

Through textual and other evidential material, as well as by reasoned argument, I have sought to establish that the Buddha could not have uttered the words attributed to him in the Pali scripture with regard to meat eating, and that he died from eating a bad mushroom and not a piece of pork. Curiously, Buddhist scholars have made no serious attempt, so far as my research discloses, to resolve the glaring discrepancies between the contentions of the two branches of Buddhism on meat eating. Perhaps they do not consider the subject weighty enough to merit their investigations, or maybe it is an issue too close to the bone—the T-bone they are loathe to give up. A number of years ago Arthur Waley did write a thoughtful paper titled, "Did Buddha Die of Eating Pork?" in which he quoted from articles by several writers on the same subject. But the larger issue of whether the Buddha did in fact sanction meat eating has been skirted even in the theses of doctoral candidates.

Yet an issue it is for many. Throughout the years people attending my workshops in the United States and abroad, as well as my formal students, have pelted me with the question, "Does Buddhism prohibit meat eating?" Except in the rare cases where the questioner's only motivation was a desire to propel themselves to center stage of the workshop, the question, I felt, was inspired not by idle curiosity but by a real personal concern. Some were unhappy about their own meat eating and wanted to know if Buddhism considered it morally wrong. For others the question was a way of seeking reassurance that flesh eating and Buddhism were compatible. For still others it was simply a desire to achieve a more humane diet. The dilemma felt by these various people was well expressed in a letter to me by a sensitive young couple, who wrote:

> We were drawn to Buddhism by its teaching of respect for all forms of life, human as well as non-human. But being new to it, we are confused and concerned about one thing. To practice Buddhism correctly, is it necessary to give up eating meat? There seems to be no agreement among Buddhists on this point. We've heard that in Japan and Southeast Asia lay Buddhists and even monks and priests eat meat, and that teachers in the United States and other Western countries do the same. But here in Rochester we're told that you and your students are vegetarians. Do the Buddhist scriptures forbid the eating of meat? If so, for what reasons? If they don't forbid it, why, may we ask, are you a vegetarian? We would become vegetarians ourselves if we were sure that by doing so we could become more deeply involved in Buddhism. But if that were not the case, we'd rather not give up meat, partly because all our friends eat it. Also, we do have some reservations from a health standpoint about a vegetarian diet.

A large part of this book has grown out of these questions.

The widespread destruction of whales, chiefly by the Japanese and the Soviets, has made these leviathans of the deep an endangered species and understandably raised hackles of alarm among environmentalists and other concerned individuals throughout the world. Since in the case of the Japanese whaling companies their actions have cynical Buddhist overtones, this issue is debated at some length toward the end of Part Two.

Five supplements have been added to the text to help dispel any doubts readers may have about the safety and desirability of adopting a meatless diet. Like an elephant, which it is said won't walk over an unknown surface until it has first tested it to be sure it will bear its weight, most people can't be persuaded to give up meat until they are convinced that their health won't suffer. In practical terms this means being reassured that a vegetarian diet can supply adequate amounts of protein. Let one say he does not eat meat and the swift reaction is, "How do you get your protein?" Thoreau's answer to a similar question is instructive. When asked by a farmer, "I hear you don't eat meat. Where do you get your strength [read 'protein']?" Thoreau, pointing to the husky team of horses drawing the farmer's wagon, replied, "Where do they get their strength?" Today, as Supplement 1 amply illustrates, one need not speculate about this issue; enlightened medical opinion affirms that with respect to protein, vegetarians are on the side of the angels.

Supplements 2 and 3 make clear that in terms of hunger, disease, and waste we pay a high price, both individually and as nations, for the dubious pleasure of ingesting the scorched carcasses of animals.

If more people were aware of the long list of eminent thinkers and humanitarians, past and present, who have adopted a vegetarian diet, and could read what these notable persons have said about the morality of abstaining from flesh food, they would realize that a vegetarian diet, far from being the province of freaks and faddists, has attracted many humane and socially concerned individuals. Hence Supplement 4.

Given the growing concern about the ethical problem of pain and violence to animals caused by their slaughter for food and widespread experimentation upon them, it is not surprising that contemporary moral philosophers and others have produced a spate of books in which they debate the vital issues of animal rights and human obligations as well as the related subjects of global famine and ecological imbalance. Most of the books in the first part of Supplement 5 deal with the moral issues of animal slaughter and flesh eating. Several excellent titles have been omitted because they are no longer in print.

Cookbooks are included in the second half for practical reasons. It is not enough to beat the drums for vegetarianism on humanitarian and ecological grounds alone. People need to be shown *how* to get started on a non-flesh diet—in other words, how to prepare delicious and nourishing meals. The hoary notion that vegetarian food is rabbit food dies hard. The recipes in the cookbooks listed have been prepared by liberated nutritionists who themselves hold to a fleshless diet. That is why they are appealing to the eye, pleasant to the taste, and nutritionally satisfying, as anyone willing to try them will discover.

A word about the illustrations. Most photographs in books dealing with animal welfare vividly portray the torment of farm and experimental animals. Their obvious purpose is to call attention to the cruelties inflicted on livestock and experimental animals and to arouse pity and sympathy for these unfortunate creatures so the reader will be moved to reflect on his own meat eating and support laws that seek to protect animals from abuse and exploitation. Such efforts, needless to say, are admirable.

The illustrations in this book have a different purpose. Consisting mainly of photographs of sculptures by well-known Chinese and Japanese artists, they are intended to emphasize the innate dignity and wholeness *(holiness)* of animals and their basic kinship with man. They affirm that "Heaven and earth and I are of the same root," as an ancient Zen master put it. To be sure, on a relative, or karmic, level human beings obviously differ from animals, even as they differ from one another, each one of us coming into this world with different physical attributes, emotional sensitivity, and intellectual capacities. But in an absolute sense, in the fundamental Buddha-nature common to all existence, we cannot speak of better or worse, higher or lower, past or future, self or other. There is no demarcation between human and animal nature.

The ancient Egyptians in particular understood this basic inseparability of the human and non-human worlds. They knew that the all-embracing One-mind is not the province of man alone but pervades all animals as well. That is why in fashioning images of the gods they mixed the human form with the figure of wild beasts. Thus the bodies of certain deities were represented in human shape, while the face and head might be that of a bird, a lion or some other animal. The ancient Chinese too understood the interrelatedness of man and beast. The Chinese sculpture of a Buddhist monk with the head of a tiger shown in the text illustrates this principle.

We need the animals: the tame for companions and to nurture and love, and wildlife to preserve the fragile balance of our ecosystem. When we destroy wildlife and its habitats we undermine the quality of our lives. As Thoreau wisely observed, "In wildness is the preservation of the world." But we need animals for other reasons. They link us with our primeval origins, and if we can establish interspecies communication, a whole new field of knowledge will open before us. The proper study of mankind is not always man, as Dr. John Lilly observed. Animals, we know, are gifted with senses and psychic powers far keener than our own and they can teach us much about our own animal nature and the mysterious world in which they move—provided we respect their uniqueness and do not patronize or exploit them. The majesty, mystery, and wonder of the animal kingdom was given classic expression by Henry Beston in his essay "Autumn, Ocean, and Birds":

> We need another wiser and perhaps a more mystical concept of animals. . . . We patronize them for their incompleteness, for their tragic fate of having taken form so far below ourselves. And therein we err. For the animal shall not be measured by man. In a world older and more complete than ours they move finished and complete, gifted with extensions of the senses we have lost or never attained, living by voices we shall never hear. They are not brethren, they are not underlings; they are other nations, caught with ourselves in the net of life and time, fellow prisoners of the splendor and travail of the earth.

Should we, though, persist in our oppression and savage destruction of our fellow earthlings, who share a common destiny with us on this imperiled planet, not only will we learn nothing from them but we will be adding to our already heavy burden of karma—a karma that one day we will have to expiate in a sea of blood and tears. For no matter what else we like to believe, one thing is certain: the law of karmic retribution cannot be outwitted.

Cow protection to me is one of the most wonderful phenomena in all human evolution, for it takes the human being beyond his species. The cow to me means the entire sub-human world. Man through the cow is enjoined to realize his identity with all that lives.... The cow is a poem of pity.... Protection of the cow means protection of the whole dumb creation of God.... The appeal of the lower order of creation is all the more forcible because it is speechless.

—*Mohandas Gandhi*

I
THE SUFFERINGS
OF ANIMALS RAISED
FOR SLAUGHTER

LET no one cherish the illusion that animals raised for slaughter by modern methods live a relatively carefree existence on the farm, with their needs amply provided for, and that when they are slaughtered it is done painlessly. The truth is just the opposite. Now that farming is largely controlled by multinational corporations and assembly-line methods of production have turned farming into agri-business, animals are treated like machines that convert low-priced fodder into high-priced flesh. These factory farms are not concerned with the welfare of the animals but with high production at low cost. With such callous attitudes dominating factory farming economics today, is it any wonder that farm animals are cruelly exploited in their rearing, their transportation to the slaughterhouse, and during the slaughtering process itself? In his influential book *Animal Liberation*, Peter Singer shows that the use and abuse of animals raised for slaughter far exceeds, in sheer numbers of animals affected, any other kind of mistreatment. The livestock industry in the United States alone raises a numbing 4 billion cattle, sheep, pigs, and chickens for slaughter each year.[4]

FACTORY FARMING OF CHICKENS

How many are aware that 95 percent of the millions of egg-laying chickens in the United States are kept under what are called "intensive" or "factory farm' stocking systems? In one common type, four hens are squeezed into what are called battery cages, 12 by 18 inches, and in this confined area they spend most of their brief lives. The cages have no perches and are made of wire mesh to allow the feces to fall through the bottom. With no solid floor to scratch on, their toenails grow very long and sometimes become entangled with the wire mesh, even causing the toe flesh itself to grow around the wire. In addition, lights in these battery cages are kept on 18 hours a day to encourage the hens to lay constantly. Each hen averages an egg every 32 hours for 14 months and then is slaughtered.

The typical egg farm in "advanced" countries today is a veritable torture chamber for its inmates. With no room to scratch the ground, build a nest, dust-bathe, stretch their wings, or even move about, the chickens' every instinct is thwarted. The inevitable stress arising from such wretched conditions drives the stronger birds to attack the weaker ones, who, with no way of escaping, may become victims of cannibalism.

To combat cannibalism, birds are de-beaked, a mutilation process whereby the beak, a complex of horn, bone, and sensitive tissue—and the chicken's most important member—is severed with either a hot knife or a guillotine-like device. Sometimes in the course of the animal's life this is done twice.[5]

THE CRUELTIES OF
OVERCROWDING AND CASTRATION

The crowding and other cruelties inflicted on pigs, one of the most commonly eaten animals in the West, are hardly less than those suffered by the roosters and hens. That the pig is an intelligent social animal doesn't save it from the abuses common to other animals raised on factory farms. Pigs that are kept in unsuitable, overcrowded conditions, as most on factory farms are, respond by biting each other's tails and fighting in general. Because this causes a reduction in their weight, farmers take oppressive remedial measures, of which cutting off the pigs' tails is one of the milder. Sows often spend several years chained to the ground in stalls too small for them to turn around in; in their craving for stimulation they will gnaw on the bars. All this brings about the "Porcine Stress Syndrome," described in one farm journal as "extreme stress . . . rigidity, blotchy skin, panting, anxiety, and often—sudden death."

Veal calves fare no better. Kept in dark, tiny stalls for sixteen weeks without enough room even to stand, they are fed a diet of no iron or roughage that wreaks havoc with their systems but keeps their flesh saleably pale.

In a general way most people are aware of numerous minor cruelties that animals on the farm suffer, whether they are reared by modern or traditional methods. It is common knowledge, for example, that nearly all cattlemen dehorn, brand, and castrate their animals, but how many reflect on the severe pain that all of these processes inflict on the animal? Even worse than dehorning and branding is castration, which most farmers admit causes shock and pain to the animal. In the United States, where anesthetics are usually not used, the procedure is to pin the animal down, take a knife, and slit the scrotum, exposing the testicles. Each testicle is then grabbed in turn and pulled on, breaking the cord that attaches it.

TERRORS OF TRANSPORTATION TO SLAUGHTER

Perhaps the greatest amount of suffering inflicted on farm animals takes place during their transportation to the slaughterhouse. Their mistreatment begins with the loading, a task often done roughly and hurriedly. Animals which in their fear and confusion have tumbled off a slick loading ramp are sometimes left unattended to slowly die of their injuries. Inside overloaded trucks the first casualties are from crushing and suffocation as a result of pile-ups. As the truck begins rolling and accelerates, often to turnpike speeds, other of the animals succumb to motion sickness.

In 1906, before trucks were used to transport animals, a federal law was passed limiting the time that animals could spend in a railway car without food or water to 28 hours, after which they had to be unloaded, fed, given water, and rested for at least 5 hours before continuing the journey. To this day no similar law has been passed, despite repeated attempts, to regulate the transport of animals by *truck*, which is how most are now shipped. Accordingly, cattle often spend not only 28 or 36 but 48 or even 72 hours inside a truck, without food or water, before being unloaded. To their desperate thirst and hunger is often added the hardships of weather; the bitter winds and cold of winter can cause severe chill, and the heat and direct sun of summer exacerbate the dehydration caused by lack of water. The suffering of the calves, which may have endured castration and the stress of weaning only a few days before, is perhaps the most acute.

EXECUTION IN THE SLAUGHTERHOUSE

Worse even than the sufferings of confinement, transportation, and other alarming aspects of the new techniques is what happens to these animals in the slaughterhouse. The process is vividly described in Upton Sinclair's *The Jungle*, a factual book about the stockyards of Chicago:

> At the same instant the ear was assailed by a most terrifying shriek... followed by another, louder and yet more agonizing—for once started upon that journey, the hog never came back. Meantime, heedless of all these things, the men upon the floor were going about their work. Neither squeals of hogs nor tears of visitors made any difference to them; one by one they hooked up the hogs, and one by one with a swift stroke they slit their throats. There was a line of hogs, with squeals and life-blood ebbing away together; until at last each started again, and vanished with a splash into a huge vat of boiling water.
>
> ...They had done nothing to deserve it; and it was adding insult to injury, as the thing was done here, swinging them up in this cold-blooded, impersonal way, without a pretense at apology, without the homage of a tear.[6]

The Jungle, it will be protested, was written many years ago; surely slaughtering is more humane today. As far as the slaughter of pigs is concerned, to judge from the following description of a visit to a slaughterhouse in modern times by a writer who grew up on a farm and was familiar with the killing of animals since childhood, the pain and terror experienced by hogs as they are led to their execution has changed little since Sinclair's time.

> The pen narrows like a funnel; the drivers behind urge the pigs forward, until one at a time they climb onto the moving ramp.... Now they scream, never having been on such a ramp, smelling the smells they smell ahead. I do not want to overdramatize because you have read all this before. But it was a frightening experience; seeing their fear, seeing so many of them go by, it had to remind me of things no one wants to be reminded of anymore, all mobs, all death marches, all mass murders and extinctions.[7]

A minister who watched a flock of sheep being led up a runway into a slaughterhouse wrote: "The smell, the cries of agony, and the noise of the killing going on inside were revolting. . . . Calves were butchered in full sight of their mothers. I watched the driving of animals to the killing floor, where they sense their fate and go mad with fear."[8]

True, in accordance with the Federal Humane Slaughter Act of 1958, some animals in the United States are stunned by electric current or a captive-bolt pistol and have their throats slit while unconscious. But these more humane methods are only required of slaughterhouses that sell meat to the federal government—a mere 10 percent of all slaughterhouses—and those in the twenty-eight states that have passed parallel legislation. This means that most of the slaughterhouses in almost half of the states are not subject to any laws or inspection regulating humane slaughter, so that they can with legal impunity resort to the use of the poleax, a heavy, long-handled sledgehammer.

The man wielding the (poleax) stands above the animal and tries to knock it unconscious with a single blow. The problem is that he must aim his long overhead swing at a moving target; for him to succeed the hammer must land at a precise point on the animal's head, and a frightened animal is quite likely to move its head. If the swing is a fraction astray, the hammer can crash through the animal's eye or nose; then, as the animal thrashes around in agony and terror, several more blows may be needed to knock it unconscious. The most skilled poleax man cannot be expected to land the blow perfectly every time. . . . It should be remembered that to make a skilled poleax man it is necessary for an unskilled poleax man to get a lot of practice. The practice will be on live animals.[9]

RITUAL SLAUGHTER

Ironically, it was religious ritual that opened another frightful loophole in the humane slaughter laws. Orthodox Jewish and Moslem dietary laws require that animals be "healthy and moving" when slaughtered (perhaps as a safeguard against diseased or unfresh meat); orthodox followers take this to mean that the animal must remain conscious until the death blow itself, which under ritual slaughter is administered with a single stroke of a knife aimed at the jugular vein and windpipe. The gruesomeness and cruelty of slaughter procedures that fulfill these requirements reach the greatest extremes in the United States, where a federal law must also be reckoned with. The Pure Food and Drug Act of 1906 stipulates that for sanitary reasons a slaughtered animal must not fall in the blood of a previously slaughtered animal. To accomplish this and still comply with kosher specifications the animal must be killed while suspended from a conveyor belt instead of lying on the slaughterhouse floor.

> Instead of being quickly knocked to the floor and killed almost as soon as they hit the ground, animals being ritually slaughtered in the United States are shackled around a rear leg, hoisted into the air, and then hang, fully conscious, upside down on the conveyor belt for between two and five minutes.... The animal, upside down, with ruptured joints and often a broken leg, twists frantically in pain and terror, so that it must be gripped by the neck or have a clamp inserted in its nostrils to enable the slaughterer to kill the animal with a single stroke, as the religious law prescribes.[10]

Those who live in an area with a large Jewish population can take little comfort in the belief that because they do not follow Jewish or Moslem dietary laws the animal whose meat they buy has not been killed in this brutal fashion. For meat to be passed as "kosher" it must also have had the blood vessels cut out of it. But since this procedure is practical for only a portion of the animal's meat, the rest usually ends up on supermarket shelves with all other non-kosher meat. Thus, far more animals have their throats slit while suspended by the leg, fully conscious, than would be necessary to meet demands for kosher meat alone.

THE COMPLICITY OF
MEAT EATERS IN ANIMAL SLAUGHTER

Because not many are acquainted with modern intensive farming methods, and fewer still have ever visited a slaughterhouse or have heard the sounds that issue from it ("Anyone who has ever heard the scream of an animal being killed," said Confucius, "could never again eat its flesh"), few people associate the ham or veal or steak they are eating with a live, suffering animal.

Others say, "Because I oppose the infliction of suffering on animals, I eat meat only from those that have not been subjected to the cruelties of either intensive farming or inhumane slaughter." In other words, it is all right to "pity and then eat the objects of one's pity." Yet it has been pointed out that, as a practical matter, it is impossible to raise animals for food on a large scale without inflicting suffering, because even if intensive methods are not employed, the traditional farming involves castration, the separation of mother and young, branding, transportation to the slaughterhouse and slaughter itself. Can anyone sincerely claim to be concerned with the welfare of animals—with the rights they undeniably have—while continuing to dine on them? Can anyone eating flesh foods, thereby indirectly aiding and abetting the oppression and killing of another creature merely to gratify his taste for a particular type of food, deny that he is making that being a means to his own end? Such a person obviously has a strong interest in convincing himself that his concern for animals need not extend as far as not eating them, as Singer points out. Yet it is only by renouncing flesh eating that one can demonstrate to himself and others that his professed concern for animals is more than empty words.

Until we boycott meat we are, each one of us, contributing to the continued existence, prosperity, and growth of factory farming and all the other cruel practices used in rearing animals for food.[11]

In the United States alone, it has been estimated, from 7 to 10 million persons abstain from flesh foods, nearly three times the number estimated a generation ago.[12] It is safe to assume that for most, vegetarianism is a protest against the slaughtering of harmless animals and a desire for a more humane diet. How can those who themselves seek emancipation from suffering inflict injury and death indirectly on other living beings by persistently eating their flesh, thereby creating a demand that can only be met by the slaughtering and butchering of these creatures?

In his book *Jean Christophe*, Romaine Rolland eloquently condemns the injustice to animals:

To a man whose mind is free, there is something even more intolerable in the suffering of animals than in the sufferings of men. For with the latter it is at least admitted that suffering is evil and that the man who causes it is a criminal. But thousands of animals are uselessly butchered every day without a shadow of remorse. If any man were to refer to it, he would be thought to be ridiculous. And that is the unpardonable crime. That alone is the justification of all that men may suffer. It cries vengeance upon all the human race. If God exists and tolerates it, it cries vengeance upon God. If there is no justice for the weak and lowly, for the poor creatures who are offered up as a sacrifice to humanity, then there is no such thing as goodness, no such thing as justice.

At this point some readers are bound to think, "Why all this concern for animals when there are millions of hungry men, women and children in the world today and thousands more who are being brutally tortured and murdered? Shouldn't our sympathy and aid be directed toward suffering humanity rather than animals?" Why must the two be separated, as though it were a matter of priorities? After all, does it take any great effort to abstain from eating the flesh of slaughtered creatures while working to create a better society for people? In the past, men like Gandhi, Tolstoy, Shaw, Upton Sinclair, and Romaine Rolland devoted their lives to improving the conditions of oppressed peoples in their respective societies. At the same time they were also highly critical of the needless slaughter of animals for food. Their concern for the decent treatment of animals did not diminish or interfere with their efforts for fair and just treatment of humans.[13]

MEAT EATING AND VIOLENCE TOWARD HUMANS

That there is a causal relationship between the cruelty, torture, and death of human beings and the ongoing slaughter of millions of pigs, cows, fowl, and sheep, not to mention whales, dolphins, and seals, must be obvious to anyone aware of the interrelation of all forms of existence and of the karmic repercussions of our actions. By our consumption of meat we allow this carnage to continue and are part perpetrators. And because of the cause-effect relationship, we are also part victims. How is it possible to swallow the carcasses of these slain creatures, permeated as they are with the violent energy of the pain and terror experienced by them at the time of their slaughter, and not have hatred, aggression, and violence stimulated in oneself and others? "While we ourselves are the living graves of murdered beasts," asks George Bernard Shaw, "how can we expect any ideal conditions on the earth?" This sentiment is echoed in an ancient Chinese verse that vividly describes the evil karma generated by the killing of animals:

> For hundreds of thousands of years
> the stew in the pot
> has brewed hatred and resentment
> that is difficult to stop.
> If you wish to know why there are disasters
> of armies and weapons in the world,
> listen to the piteous cries
> from the slaughterhouse at midnight.

The salvation
Of birds and beasts, oneself included—
This is the object
Of Shakyamuni's[14] religious austerities.

—*Zen Master Ikkyu*

II

MEAT EATING
AND
THE FIRST PRECEPT

IN Buddhism the first precept[15] of not killing, or harmlessness to living beings (*fu-sessho* in Japanese, *ahimsa* in Sanskrit) has a religious rather than a moral or metaphysical basis. By this I mean that it is grounded in our Buddha-nature[16]—the matrix of all phenomena—from which arises our sense of compassion and moral goodness. Or to put it another way, this precept is based on the principle of mutual attraction and rightness common to all nature. The same can be said for the other cardinal precepts, each of which can be thought of as an extension or different aspect of the first precept. It is in Buddha-nature that all existences, animate and inanimate, are unified and harmonized. All organisms seek to maintain this unity in terms of their own karma. To willfully take life, therefore, means to disrupt and destroy this inherent wholeness and to blunt feelings of reverence and compassion arising from our Buddha-mind. The first precept of not killing is really a call to life and creation even as it is a condemnation of death and destruction.

Deliberately to shoot, knife, strangle, drown, crush, poison, burn, electrocute or otherwise intentionally take the life of a living being or to purposefully inflict pain on a human being or animal—these are not the only ways to defile this precept. To cause *another* to kill, torture, or harm any living creature likewise offends against the first precept. Thus to put the flesh of an animal into one's belly makes one an accessory after the fact of its slaughter, simply because if cows, pigs, sheep, fowl, and fish, to mention the most common, were not eaten they would not be killed.

Although it is true that in Mahayana Buddhism the culpability for taking life involves various considerations, these need not concern us here, for with the exception of hunters, slaughterers, and fishermen, who kill the food they eat, the majority of flesh eaters are only indirectly responsible for the violence to and destruction of animals. This, however, does not make them any less answerable to the first precept.

Yasutani-roshi has pointed out in his book on the precepts why it is important to uphold the precept of not-killing:

> These days many voices proclaim the sanctity of human life. Human life should of course be valued highly, but at the same time the lives of other living beings should also be treasured. Human beings snatch away the lives of other creatures whenever it suits their purposes. The way of thinking that encourages this behavior arises from a specifically human brand of violence that defies the self-evident laws of the universe, opposes the growth of the myriad things in nature, and destroys feelings of compassion and reverence arising from our Buddha-nature. In view of such needless destruction of life, it is essential that laymen and monks together conscientiously uphold this precept.[17]

The first precept has another religious aspect. Buddhism teaches that there is not a single being that has not been our mother, our father, husband, wife, sister, brother, son or daughter in its ascent and descent of the ladder of cause and effect through countless rebirths—not one being whose kinship with us even while in the animal state has not continued. How then can one who approaches all living things as though they were himself eat the flesh of something that is of the same nature as himself and not be guilty of cannibalism of a sort? Or to put it another way, since our Buddha-nature assumes many forms, the creature that is a cow today may in a future rebirth become a human being and from that state realize its innate perfection—that is, become Buddha.[18] From this emerges the distinctly Buddhist notion that *all* life, human and non-human, is sacred. This does not mean that human beings are to be treated like cows and cows like human beings; clearly each has different capabilities and different needs. What it does mean is that in a just society the rights of non-humans are not ignored or trampled upon.

BUDDHIST AND CHRISTIAN VIEWS OF ANIMALS

From the foregoing it is obvious that Buddhists do not understand the first precept in the same way that Christians and Jews understand the commandment in the Decalogue of Moses not to take life. And also unlike the Judeo-Christian religions, Buddhism does not place man at the pinnacle of creation. Rather, he occupies a place halfway between the most bound (hellish) condition and the most emancipated (a full Buddha); or to state it in a less traditional way, midway between base ignorance and complete enlightenment. Nor does Buddhism endow man with an immortal soul that is destined to reside either in eternal bliss in a heaven or in eternal damnation in a hell. In common with other creatures, human beings are constantly advancing toward complete self-realization or falling back towards hellish states according to causes and conditions—according to their karma.

Once the Judeo-Christian religions, in an exuberance of self-deification, elevated man to the status of the lord of creation, it was a short step to giving him the power of life and death over non-human beings. In the words of the Bible:

...And God said, Let us make man in our image, after our likeness: and let them have dominion over the fish of the sea and over the birds of the air, and over the cattle, and over all the earth, and over every creeping thing that creeps upon the earth.... And God said to them, Be fruitful and multiply, and fill the earth and subdue it....

And God blessed Noah and his sons, and said to them...The fear of you and the dread of you shall be upon every beast of the earth, and upon every bird of the air, upon everything that creeps on the ground and all the fish of the sea; into your hands they are delivered....

For environmentalist and social critic Ian McHarg, for historians Arnold Toynbee and Lynn White, Jr., and for other thoughtful persons those fateful words of the Bible have determined the destructive course of Western civilization for 2,000 years. In a lecture which he gave several years ago at Queens University in Kingston, Ontario, in a series examining the question of Western man's attitude to the natural world, McHarg had this to say of the biblical injunction:

Now, if you want to find one text of compounded horror which will guarantee that the relationship of man to nature can only be

destruction, which will atrophy any creative skill, then you do not have to look any further. If you want to find one text which if believed and employed literally, or simply accepted implicitly, without the theological origins being known, will explain all of the destruction and all of the despoliation accomplished by Western man for at least these 2,000 years, then you do not have to look any further than this ghastly, calamitous text.

With divine sanction to dominate and subdue all the creatures of the earth, is it any wonder that man, who considers himself the highest creation of God, ignores the right of non-humans to share this universe with him, oppressing and destroying them at his whim by convincing himself that his well-being requires their slaughter? How can any society speak of justice or mercy when it needlessly butchers defenseless creatures unable to speak out against their oppression? How can any spiritual person who himself seeks liberation from suffering persistently eat the flesh of animals, thereby causing them to suffer the pain and terror entailed in their slaughter?

DID THE BUDDHA DIE FROM EATING MEAT ?

In view of the first precept's prohibition against causing another to take life, it is appropriate to inquire how meat-eating Buddhist priests, monks, and teachers justify such a transgression. Question them and they are sure to say, "Don't you know that the Buddha himself ate a piece of pork offered him at the home of one of his followers? Although normally he did not eat flesh foods, his sense of gratitude would not permit him to refuse it. Like the Buddha, we gratefully eat whatever is put before us, without preference or aversion." (The "meat," it turned out, was putrid and it poisoned the Buddha, causing his death.) And then they will add, "And are you not also aware that the Buddha laid down the rule that one must refrain from eating meat only if one knows, hears, or suspects the animal has been killed specifically for one's own consumption?"

These versions of what the Buddha is supposed to have done and said one hears in Japan, in Burma, in Sri Lanka, in Nepal, and in Thailand, but, significantly, not in India, China, Singapore, nor among Indian and Chinese Buddhists in North America. How reliable are they? This point is important, because monks, teachers and lay people have taken refuge in these supposed actions and statements of the Buddha to justify their meat eating, implying that if the Buddha himself ate flesh food when it was offered him, surely they have warrant to do likewise. What they gloss over with respect to the first proposition is the research of scholars, the majority of whom contend that it was not a piece of meat but a poisonous truffle (a species of mushroom) that caused the Buddha's death; and what they ignore with respect to the second are the Mahayana scriptures, which unequivocally condemn meat eating.

Let us first consider the "pork-eating" incident. In *Dialogues of the Buddha*, translated from the Pali by Mr. and Mrs. Rhys Davids, we find the following passage:

> . . . Then Chunda addressed the Exalted One and said, "May the Exalted One do me the honor of taking his meal, together with the brethren, at my house tomorrow?"
> And the Exalted One signified by his silence his consent. . . .
> Now at the end of the night, Chunda, the worker in metals, made ready in his dwelling place sweet rice and cakes, and a quantity of truffles.[19]

The word translated as "truffles" is *sukara-maddava*. Arthur Waley, in his article "Did the Buddha Die of Eating Pork?" says that *sukara-maddava* has at least four interpretations: (1) a pig's soft food, i.e., food eaten by pigs, (2) "pig's delight," i.e., a favorite food of pigs, (3) the soft parts of a pig, or (4) "pig-pounded," i.e., food trampled by pigs.[20] The scholar K.E. Neumann, Waley says,

> has shown that in Narahari's *Rajanighantu*, among the names of medical plants, there occurs a whole series of compound words having 'pig' as their first element; thus *sukara-kanda*, 'pig-bulb'; *sukara-padika*, 'pig's foot; *sukareshta*, 'sought-out by pigs'. On the analogy of the last, Neumann takes *sukaramaddava* to mean 'pig's delight,' and assumes that it is the name of some kind of truffles.

Waley further points out:

> Plant names tend to be local and dialectical. It is quite likely that if such an expression as *sukaramaddava* meant "truffles" in Maghada, it might, in the more western and southern centres where Pali Buddhism came into existence, have been entirely unknown and consequently misunderstood.

Significantly, Edward Thomas, referring to the controversial *sukara-maddava* in his *The Life of Buddha*, notes, "The word, however, is not the obvious *sukaramamsa*, 'pig flesh,' which we would expect if this were meant."[21] Mrs. Rhys Davids, in her *A Manual of Buddhism*, casts the "pig's flesh" interpretation into further doubt when she observes:

> A food-compound of pig-flesh *(sukaramamsa)* does occur once in the scriptures, in a sutta of a curiously unworthy kind, where a householder, in inviting Gotama to dine, goes through quite a menu in a refrained detail! *Maddava* is nowhere else associated with meat, and I remain of Rhys Davids' opinion that we have here a dish...of a root, such as truffles, much sought by swine, and which may have been called "pig's joy." Such a root we actually have—this the critics did not know—in our "pignut,"...the little nut-shaped bulbous roots of which, called also "earthnuts," are liked by both pigs and children.[22]

Laying aside scholarship, what reasonable person can believe that Chunda offered the Buddha a piece of pork when the latter came to pay him a visit? As one of the Buddha's followers, surely he would have known that flesh food was not part of the Buddha's diet. (Very likely Chunda didn't eat meat himself, as most Indians still don't today.) Why, then, would he have offered meat to the World-Honored One, a person so sensitive to the sufferings of all living beings that he would not drink milk from a cow during the first ten days after its calf was born?

MEAT OFFERING AS ALMS

Anyone who has ever been on takuhatsu (i.e., going forth to proclaim the Dharma[23] and receiving alms), or been invited more than once to meals at the homes of believers knows that in almost all cases these persons offer priests and teachers foods they have been made aware the latter like to eat. Especially in the case of a *roshi*,[24] the hostess will make a point of asking his attendant or others in advance of his coming what kind of food he normally eats so that she can please him with her offering, or at least not serve him food that does not agree with him physically or spiritually. Even in the Buddha's day would-be donors of meals to the Buddha often consulted Ananda, his attendant.[25]

Whenever I had a meal in the company of either my teacher Harada-roshi or my teacher Yasutani-roshi, neither of whom I saw eat flesh foods, we were never served fish or meat. But on a takuhatsu led by a roshi who loved fish or meat, the dinner table groaned with these foods.

That hosts cater to the preferences, or supposed preferences, of the monks or laypeople to whom they donate a meal was painfully brought home to me on my first takuhatsu in Japan. After the monks and I had traveled by train to a town distant from the monastery and then marched around the town all day crying "Ho" (Dharma) as we received monetary offerings and uncooked rice and vegetables, we arrived at the home of the believer who was to donate our meal. After chanting sutras in memory of the family dead we sat down to dinner. Instead of the gleaming dishes of fish, eggs, *sushi*,[26] and bottles of saké and beer that were set in front of the roshi[27] and the monks, I was dismayed to find confronting me a large steak with french-fried potatoes, a jigger of whiskey, and black coffee. Not certain whether these gastronomic ghosts of a painful past were intended as some sort of Zen test, yet not wanting to appear ungrateful, I bravely downed the whiskey neat, then tackled the steak, washing it down with the coffee. Several hours later I reaped the karmic[28] retribution of this folly: a badly aching belly. When the opportunity came to speak with the roshi about this, I asked him, "Why wasn't I served the same food and drink as the others?"

"These simple villagers," he explained, "have the idea that all Americans like steak, whiskey, and black coffee. To show their admiration for your efforts in Buddhism, they offered you food and drink they thought you would enjoy. You would offend them if you didn't eat any of it."

That explanation mitigated my anxiety but not my American karma, for at the next takuhatsu once more I alone was offered the inevitable steak accompanied by whiskey and black coffee. Now, however, fish was added. I ate this in its entirety but merely nibbled at the steak and sipped the coffee and liquor. Result? Another pain in the belly. Clearly it was time to appeal to higher authority, so I took the matter up with the abbot, Harada-roshi. "If even in the United States," I told him, "I avoided such food and drink because they caused me digestive difficulties, why do I have to eat them on takuhatsu?"

"Don't eat anything that doesn't agree with you!" he commanded, his tone brooking of no compromise. The word from on high evidently spread quickly to the rank and file of temple supporters, for at the meal donated at the next takuhatsu, fish and rice replaced the steak and french fries, and saké and tea prevailed over whiskey and coffee. All this I ate with as much relish as the monks. Not only was the fish a relief from the dreary three meals a day of rice (buttressed at noontime with miso soup and a few vegetables); it also served to allay my fears of insufficient protein—ah, yes, protein, the great American bugaboo (see Supplement 1)!

MEAT IN THE DIET OF JAPANESE MONKS

Although none of the monasteries where I trained ever formally served meat, fish, or poultry, few monks dispensed with these foods even when they were in training. If they didn't get flesh food during takuhatsu or at the homes of friends, they got it when the abbot left town. At such times one or two of them would take up a collection among the monks, then bike to town and surreptitiously buy the special beef required for *sukiyaki*, their favorite meat dish. Temple supporters did their share in helping the monks besmirch the first precept by providing ample quantities of prepared fish and meats during certain monastery celebrations or ceremonies. Only a monk with an ailing stomach or uncommon courage would have dared refuse such largess.

So many monk-trainees ate fish and meat when it was made available to them that few had the faintest notion why the monastery kitchen did not provide flesh foods. Once early in my training I asked a young monk who spoke good English, "Why don't we ever get beef, fish, or chicken?" "Because," he replied, "the monastery can't afford those foods." At the time that explanation seemed plausible. But the same question put by me to one of the head monks at a later time elicited quite a different reponse: "Meat stimulates the passions, and obviously such stimulation would not help the practice of the monks. Besides, meat, especially if eaten in large quantities, leads to irritability and aggression; that is another reason why the monastery does not serve it."

"What about milk?" I asked. "Why doesn't the monastery keep cows? Wouldn't the monks be healthier drinking milk and eating butter and cheese?"

"There are many reasons for not keeping cows at a Zen monastery," he explained, "but mainly we do not drink milk here for the same reason that the Buddha himself did not drink it; it deprives the calves of it."[29] That last remark set me to thinking about my own milk drinking, but since he stopped short of condemning the consumption of meat and fish as depriving harmless animals of their lives—how could he condemn them when he was still dining on them at times himself?—the connection of flesh eating with the first precept never hit home.

Somehow it had never occurred to me that eating flesh foods led to the unnecessary killing of innocent animals. Perhaps there was an excuse for my unawareness. In the few talks on the first precept of not-killing that the roshi gave I can't ever remember his making that connection. Once or twice when I asked senior monks whether the Buddha had actually sanctioned meat eating, they blithely assured me that he forbade it only when one had reason to believe the animal whose flesh was being offered had been killed expressly for oneself.

FLESH EATING IN A
SOUTHEAST ASIAN MONASTERY

If the procuring and eating of fish and meat in the Japanese monasteries has a sleight-of-hand quality, in those of Southeast Asia monks and lay perseons eat flesh foods openly and unabashedly, evidently in the "innocent" belief that no violation of the first precept is involved. At least this seemed true in one large Buddhist monastery outside Rangoon, in Burma, where I spent five weeks as a lay monk in the late 1950's. Each morning at 6:30 the driver of my sponsor (who had undertaken, as an act of merit, to supply my food for the entire period of my stay) pulled up in a jeep to my room and deposited a huge quantity of food that was to be downed before 12 noon, the bewitching hour. In Theravada Buddhism *when* you eat is more important than *what* you eat, and when I entered the monastery I like everyone else had to sign a pledge to observe the first five precepts and not to eat solid food beyond noon. Woe to the monk or layman (in the monastery) who transgressed this rule!

My day's rations usually consisted of two legs of fried chicken, potatoes, bread, fruit, cake, and coffee. Conspicuously missing were native curries, rice, and fish. Here was a cuisine obviously intended to please the palate of a Westerner. But so large was the quantity brought me that I returned half of it when the driver came to pick up the trays at 11:30. The next day with the food came this note from my sponsor: "Food should not be wasted. All of it is for you. Please eat it."

To consume all this food before noon would mean, in practice, eating what would add up to four ordinary meals in five hours—a feat impossible for me to accomplish without ending up with a stomach ache. Nor would it have been any easier were we required to do some manual work beyond sweeping our own room each day. So at the risk of incurring the displeasure of my sponsor, I "donated" most of it to the many dogs inhabiting the monastery compound. The dogs had other benefactors as well. Occupying rooms in the same bungalow where I had a room were a number of judges and lawyers from the high court in Rangoon who had "taken the robe" for a 3-week period that embraced the Burman New Year, when it was considered particularly meritorious to be in the monastery since it meant foregoing the convivial celebrations most Burmans were engaging in on the outside.

Each day the wives of these quasi-monks, all nattily attired, drove up to the monastery with their spouses' food. Accompanying them were their children, who chatted with their fathers while their mothers served up curries and other Burman dishes, including meat and fish. And since the wives, too, brought more food than their husbands could consume before noon, a sizeable portion of it, consisting mostly of rice and bread (but not meat or fish), went to the dogs.

Can such widespread eating of flesh foods be reconciled with the first precept of not-killing and harmlessness to living beings? "Certainly," say those who justify their meat eating by citing the purported words of the Buddha sanctioning flesh eating. What, then, are the words attributed to the Buddha and how believable is it that he uttered them?

DID THE BUDDHA SANCTION MEAT EATING? THERAVADA VERSION

In the Jivaka Sutta the Buddha is addressed by one Jivaka, who says he's heard it said that people slay animals expressly "for the recluse Gotama, who wittingly eats meat expressly meant for him and deliberately provided for him." After stating that he is being misrepresented, the Buddha is quoted as saying:

. . .I forbid the eating of meat in three cases—if there is evidence either of your eyes or of your ears or if there are grounds of suspicion.[30]

And in three cases I allow it—if there is no evidence either of your
eyes or of your ears and if there be no grounds of suspicion. . .

I.B. Horner in her booklet *Early Buddhism and the Taking of
Life* interprets the words attributed to the Buddha in this wise:

Monks were allowed to eat meat and fish provided that it was
"pure" in three respects, which meant a monk had neither seen,
heard, nor suspected that it had been killed on purpose for him. . . [31]

After pointing out that the bloody trades of butchering, hunting, and fishing are condemned by early Buddhism, she writes:

Although the eating of meat by laity and monks alike is tacitly
condoned, the bloody trades which bring animals to destruction
for this purpose by no means escape condemnation. . .

And it [Buddhism's advocacy of non-injury] may have been
due to the presumption that animals have as much right to their
lives, and to compassion, as have human beings.

Horner stands logic and common sense on its head when
she says in one breath that the first precept of non-injury in Buddhism arises from the presumption that animals have as much
right to their lives as have human beings, and in the next affirms
that the Buddha "tacitly condoned" meat eating and, by implica-
tion, the suffering and destruction of animals.

Even more incomprehensible is her linking the word "pure"
with meat eating. There has never been a genuine spiritual
master either before, during, or after the Buddha's time who has
defended meat eating or denied that it is a bar to realization of
the highest states of spirituality.[32] Why? Because meat stimulates
the lower passions, causing restlessness and dis-ease; it is
psychically disturbing; and it contains toxins generated by the
fear and terror experienced by the animal at the time of
slaughter.

How plausible is it that the Buddha sanctioned the eating of
animal flesh by his monks in all circumstances except when they
had reason to suspect the animal had been killed specifically for
them? Aren't domestic animals slaughtered for whoever eats
their meat? If no one ate their flesh, obviously they would not be
killed, so how can there be a distinction between "It was not killed specifically for me" and "It was killed for me"? Can anyone
imagine a bhikku (monk) saying to his host who had offered him
meat, "Sir, it is kind of you to donate this food to me, but as I have

reason to believe the animal from which it came was killed just for me, I cannot accept it"! Actually, how many donors even in the Buddha's day had a pig or cow butchered *just* for a certain monk? Few indeed. And this would be even less true today. So if the Buddha actually uttered the statements attributed to him, what they would mean effectively is that with the exception of the handful of persons who were offered meat from an animal killed just for them—and of course hunters, slaughterers, and fishermen—he freely sanctioned meat eating for everyone, including his monks. Not only does this contention fly in the face of the first precept, which makes one who causes another to take life equally culpable; it also implies that the Buddha approved of butchering and the horrors of the slaughterhouse. Yet slaughtering is one of the trades forbidden to Buddhists, and with good reason. To say on the one hand that the Buddha sanctioned flesh eating in all cases except those already noted, and on the other that he condemned the bloody trades of slaughtering, hunting, and trapping, not only denies the link between the two, it involves one in an absurd contradiction.

Who else but meat eaters are responsible for the perpetuation of the "bloody trades" of butchering, hunting, and fishing? After all, the slaughterers, and the meat-packing houses that sustain them, are only responding to the demands of the flesh eaters. "I'm only doing your dirty work," was the reply of a slaughterer to a gentleman who was objecting to the brutality of the slaughterhouse. "It's such as you makes such as us."[33] Every individual who eats flesh food, whether an animal is killed expressly for him or not, is supporting the trade of slaughtering and contributing to the violent deaths of harmless animals. Was the Buddha so obtuse that he failed to understand this—he who has been described as "a Perfect One, in whom all spiritual, mental, and psychic faculties have come to perfection...and whose consciousness encompasses the infinity of the universe"? Was he so unperceptive that he didn't realize that only by abstaining from flesh foods can one effectively end both the killing of defenseless animals and the infliction of suffering upon them?

Yet in a profound sense all of us, meat eaters and vegetarians alike, must share responsibility for this violence and suffering. The "brand of the slaughterhouse is on the brow of all of us," as Henry Salt observed many years ago.

The Buddha, we are told, forbade his monks to eat the flesh of such animals as elephants, dogs, lions, tigers, bears, and hyenas. Now, if monks are supposed to receive all food without preferences or aversion, and would-be donors are free to donate whatever food they wish, why should the Buddha sanction the eating of one kind of flesh food and condemn another? Does a pig or cow, whose meat is supposedly approved for eating, suffer any less pain when it is slaughtered than a dog or bear? Was the Buddha less sensitive than Rousseau when the latter wrote in his *Emile*:

> The animals you eat are not those who devour others; you do not eat the carnivorous beasts, you take them as your pattern. You only hunger for the sweet and gentle creatures which harm no one, which follow you, serve you, and are devoured by you as the reward of their service.

Or less empathetic than Voltaire when he penned these words: "What barbarian is there who would cause a lamb to be butchered and roasted if that lamb conjured him, in an effecting appeal, not to be at once assassin and cannibal?"[34]

Anyone familiar with the numerous accounts of the Buddha's extraordinary compassion and reverence for living beings—for example, his insistence that his monks carry filters to strain the water they drink lest they inadvertently cause the death of any micro-organisms in the water[35]—could never believe that he would be indifferent to the sufferings of domestic animals caused by their slaughter for food.

More reasonably, we would expect the Buddha to forbid his monks to eat *every* kind of animal flesh. After all, the Vinaya (the book of discipline governing monks' behavior) was intended principally, if not exclusively, for the use of monks and for their moral welfare. If, as Horner points out, "The monk world had a different code from the lay-world...one of as complete non-harming as it was possible to achieve," surely the Buddha could demand of his monks what he could not demand of his lay followers, namely, abstention from all flesh foods. Why was that so impossible? Monks by virtue of their training, their strength of character, and their life purpose are different—stronger if you like—than lay people and presumably better able to resist the pleasures of the senses to which ordinary persons succumb. Indeed, that is why they renounce sexual pleasure and do not eat beyond twelve noon. Now, were they to eat solid food in the afternoon or evening, whom would they be hurting except possibly themselves? But if they ate the more (by ordinary standards) delectable meat of cows, pigs, chickens, and sheep, not only are they indulging themselves in the manner of lay persons but, even worse, they are indirectly causing pain and death to other living creatures and perpetrating morally indefensible acts. Why, it has to be asked, should the taking of solid food after noontime be a more serious offense than eating animal flesh? Clearly something is rotten in the state of Magadha, and there is no escaping the question: Did the Buddha really say the things the compilers of the Pali suttas would have us believe he said on the subject of meat eating?

MAHAYANA VERSION

He did not—if one believes the words attributed to him in the Mahayana sutras: the *Lankavatara*, the *Surangama*, the *Mahaparinirvana*, and the *Brahmajala*, all of which clearly and unmistakably condemn meat eating. Consider, for example, these extracts from the *Lankavatara*, which devotes an entire chapter to the evils of eating flesh food:

> For the sake of love of purity, the Bodhisattva should refrain from eating flesh, which is born of semen, blood, etc. For fear of causing terror to living beings let the Bodhisattva, who is disciplining himself to attain compassion, refrain from eating flesh. . .
>
> It is not true that meat is proper food and permissible when the animal was not killed by himself, when he did not order others to kill it, when it was not specially meant for him. . . Again, there may be some people in the future who. . . being under the influence of the taste for meat will string together in various ways sophistic arguments to defend meat eating. . .
>
> But. . . meat eating in any form, in any manner, and in any place is unconditionally and once for all prohibited. . . Meat eating I have not permitted to anyone, I do not permit, I will not permit. . . . [36]

And these words from the Surangama sutra:

> The reason for practicing dhyana[37] and seeking to attain Samadhi[38] is to escape from the suffering of life, but in seeking to escape from suffering ourselves why should we inflict it upon others? Unless you can so control your minds that even the thought of brutal

unkindness and killing is abhorrent, you will never be able to escape from the bondage of the world's life...After my Parinirvana[39] in the last kalpa[40] different kinds of ghosts will be encountered everywhere deceiving people and teaching them that they can eat meat and still attain enlightenment...How can a bhikshu, who hopes to become a deliverer of others, himself be living on the flesh of other sentient beings?[41]

The *Mahaparinirvana Sutra* (Mahayana version) states: "The eating of meat extinguishes the seed of great compassion."

How is it that the Mahayana teachings directly contradict those of the Theravada in the matter of meat eating? Some commentators attribute the difference to a shift in public morality that took place in the years between the compiling of the two sets of scriptures. But this contention faces two objections. First, it overlooks the fact that even before the Buddha's time the scriptures of the various spiritual traditions in India condemned flesh eating as not conducive to spiritual progress. Secondly, as Conze and other scholars have pointed out, many of the Sanskrit scriptures were contemporary, or nearly so, with the Pali (Theravada). Isn't it reasonable to suppose that if the elders of the Mahayana were satisfied that the Theravada suttas correctly reflected the Buddha's views as respects meat eating, they would have remained silent on this point? That they spoke out, and vehemently so, shows how deeply disturbed they were by what they obviously felt was a distortion of his teaching and a corruption of the spirit and intent of the first precept.

On the subject of ahimsa (harmlessness to living beings), the *Encyclopaedia of Buddhism* points out:

In China and Japan the eating of meat was looked upon as an evil and was ostracised...The eating of meat gradually ceased [around 517] and this tended to become general. It became a matter of course not to use any kind of meat in the meals of temples and monasteries.[42]

In Japan up until the middle of the 19th century, when Buddhism was still a vital force in the lives of the Japanese, meat eating was a taboo; Japan was essentially a vegetarian country.[43] For a Buddhist monk, much less a roshi, to consume even fish would earn him the contemptuous *namagusubozu!*—"you unholy monk smelling of raw fish!"

The diary of Zen master Dogen, written while he was in

China in the 13th century, contains further evidence of the strictness of the ban against meat eating in China. Dogen asked his teacher Ju-ching, "What must the mental attitude and daily activities of a student be when he is engaged in Buddhist meditation and practice?" Ju-ching answered that one of the things he should avoid, especially if he is a beginner, is eating meat.[44]

Coming down to modern times, Holmes Welch, an authority of Chinese Buddhism, points out that:

> Chinese monks who abstained from meat were able to perform rites for the dead with greater effectiveness. If lay people knew that meat was being eaten at a monastery, it was less likely to receive their patronage...This accounts for the complaints of foreign travelers in China that monks would not allow them even to pass the night at their temples because of the fear that meat might be smuggled in and eaten on the premises...[45]

Alexandra David-Neel, who spent many years in Tibet, tells us that while Tibetans in general are fond of meat, many lamas entirely abstain from animal food, and if they eat meat or not, all except followers of Tantric[46] doctrines declare that meat eating is an evil action which brings harmful results to those who are guilty of it and "creates a deleterious psychic atmosphere in places where it is habitually eaten."[47] She also says that in the Sagain Mountains in Burma she has known whole communities of bhikkus (ordained members of the Order) who were strictly vegetarian. Surely this shows that even in Theravadin countries not all monks and lay people subscribed to the Pali version of what the Buddha supposedly said about meat eating. She also points out that there were many pious laymen who imitated them in Tibet. The Tibet she is speaking of is of course the one she knew before the Chinese invasion and annexation. In that Tibet, she adds, it was usual to abstain from meat on the days of Buddhist observances three times a month: on the day of the new moon, on the last day of the month, and especially on the 15th of the month.

THE DOCTRINE OF AHIMSA IN INDIA

To further show the improbability of the Buddha's having uttered the words attributed to him in the Pali texts as respects meat eating, let us explore briefly the doctrine of ahimsa in India and its pervasiveness in the Indian religious consciousness. As far

back as the Vedas[48] and Upanishads,[49] which antedate the Buddha, strictures against meat eating are numerous. Dr. Koshelya Walli in her book *The Conception of Ahimsa in Indian Thought* points out that while meat eating was not unknown in ancient times, the scriptures unanimously condemn the practice. She quotes them to this effect:

> Meat can never be obtained without injuring creatures, and injury to sentient beings is detrimental to heavenly bliss; therefore, one should shun meat eating. . .
>
> One should consider the disgusting origin of flesh and the cruelty of fettering and slaying corporeal beings, and entirely abstain from flesh eating. . .
>
> He who permits the slaughter of animals, he who cuts up, kills, buys, sells, cooks, serves it up and eats—every one of these is a slayer of animals. . .
>
> He who seeks to increase his own flesh with the flesh of others, not worshipping the gods or manes, is the greatest of all sinners. . .
>
> Meat cannot be obtained from straw or stone. It can be obtained only by slaughtering a creature, hence meat is not to be eaten. . .
>
> Others should be treated as one's own self and should be protected as such. . . [50]

The teaching of ahimsa strongly influenced the spiritual climate of the Buddha's day. Mahavira, the founder of Jainism and a contemporary of the Buddha, considered harmlessness to all living things the sublimest of virtues and made it a fundamental tenet of his teaching. The Jain respect for life can be seen in these extracts from the Acaranga sutra:

> All beings with two, three, four, or five senses. . .in fact all creation, know individually pleasure and displeasure, pain, terror, and sorrow. All are full of fears which come from all directions. And yet there exist people who would cause greater pain to them. . .Some kill animals for sacrifice, some for their skin, flesh, blood. . .feathers, teeth, or tusks. . .some kill them intentionally and some unintentionally; some kill because they have been previously injured by them. . .and some because they expect to be injured. He who harms animals has not understood or renounced deeds of sin. . .Those whose minds are at peace and who are free from passions do not desire to live at the expense of others. . .[51]

Ahimsa and the name Ashoka, the famous Buddhist emperor of India (268-233 B.C.), are indissolubly linked. Before his conversion to Buddhism, Ashoka, a rapacious conqueror, caused the cruel deaths of thousands of human beings. After he adopted the teachings of the Buddha, the wholesale destruction of men *and* animals in his empire ceased and relative peace prevailed. He prohibited the sacrifice of animals as offerings and restricted the eating of meat. "I have enforced the law against killing certain animals and many others," he declared in one of his Pillar Edicts, "but the greatest progress of Righteousness among men comes from the exhortation in favor of non-injury to life and abstention from killing living beings."[52]

One can judge how deeply the doctrine of ahimsa had penetrated into the Indian consciousness from this picture of India given us at the beginning of the 5th century by Fa-hsien, the famous Chinese Buddhist pilgrim:

> The inhabitants are numerous and happy...Throughout the country the people *do not kill any living creature,* nor drink intoxicating liquor...they do not keep pigs and fowl, and do not sell live cattle; in the markets *there are no butcher shops* and no dealers in intoxicating drink...Only the Chandalas [the lowest and most despised caste] are fishermen and hunters and sell flesh meat...[emphasis added][53]

On a pilgrimage to India in the 1950's I marveled at the same phenomenon of the absence of butcher shops and liquor stores. India is a vegetarian's delight. It is not that the Indians can't afford flesh foods, but that every great spiritual figure in India—including in modern times Mohandas Gandhi—so emphasized non-violence and harmlessness to living beings that even wealthy Indians spurn animal flesh. The unique Indian reverence and gratitude toward the cow, the surrogate mother of the human race, should therefore come as no surprise. While other "civilized" nations butcher the docile cow when she can no longer give them milk, Indians protect her by according her the status of sacred. It is to the everlasting credit of Gandhi that even in the face of much opposition he resolutely defended the protection of cows.

DENIGRATION OF MEAT ANIMALS

In heavy meat-consuming countries, where unproductive cows by the millions are routinely slaughtered for food, these animals receive anything but reverence and gratitude. A gentleman farmer whom I once heard needling a swami expressed the prevalent attitude toward them in these words: "Why do you Indians treat the cow as sacred? Don't you know it's one of the dumbest animals alive, good only for giving milk and eating?" Just as we slander people we have wronged by attaching to them such labels as "congenitally lazy," "stupid," "dirty," or "barbarous" to justify our oppression and/or exploitation of them, in the same way we denigrate animals we want to slaughter in order to eat them with an untroubled conscience. And so the pig, which is a relatively clean animal, is labeled "dirty swine," the cow "bovine"—a term implying stupidity and unfeelingness—and the whale, "killer." (Is there a more pervasive killer than civilized man?) On top of that we invent euphemisms like "ham," "pork," "steak," "beef," "veal," and "mutton" so we won't be reminded that we are ingesting the scorched flesh of dead pigs, cows, calves, and sheep, slain for the pleasures of our palates. In fact the word "meat" itself is a euphemism. Originally referring to solid food, as in the expression "meat and drink," it later came to mean the flesh of an animal. Oddly enough, it retains its original meaning in the term "nut meat."

Buddhism is not a religion of dumb acquiescence or blind belief. In one of his most salient utterances the Buddha urged his followers not to believe solely in the written words of some wise man, or in the mere authority of one's teachers or priests, but to accept as true whatever agrees with one's own reason and experience, after thorough investigation, and whatever helps oneself and other living beings. Applying the Buddha's yardstick and taking into account his character and the religious atmosphere of his time, is it more reasonable to accept the strict rejection of flesh eating of the Mahayana or the waffling permissiveness of the Theravada?

THE PALI CANON ON MEAT EATING

Still, a question remains. How did those words imputed to the Buddha get into the Pali canon? The answer is simple: Monks and scribes still attached to meat eating put them there. Sound far fetched, does it? Then consider how the suttas, and the Vinaya in particular, came into being. For at least a hundred years after the Buddha's *parinirvana* the discourses, dialogues, monastic regulations, verses, stories, and plays were handed down orally—in the case of the Vinaya, 300 years later, according to the Buddhist scholar Rhys Davids. That is to say, they were memorized by the different schools of Buddhism at the time and spoken in both metric and fixed prose form, so inevitably differences developed. Neither the Pali suttas nor the Mahayana sutras was "revealed" at one time and in one place. The Buddhist canon, Mr. and Mrs. Rhys Davids assure us, is no different from any of the other ancient religious literature of the world in that it developed gradually to become "a mosaic of earlier and later material."

Each sutta begins with the tried-and-true formula "Thus have I heard," implying that the words that follow are not the author's but the Buddha's. Commendable modesty! But also a polemic device for conferring authenticity on the writers' statements by attributing them to the Buddha.

After the Buddha's passing, three councils were held over a hundred years to establish the Buddhist canon, that is, to determine what material was "legitimate" and what was not. Obviously the councils entailed much discussion, selection, and emendation. Can anyone doubt that throughout this period the utterances of the Buddha, or those attributed to him, were expanded, subtracted, rewritten, recopied, and arranged to suit the tastes, dispositions and interpretations of the elders of the various Buddhist schools who took part in this lengthy process?

Leading Buddhist scholars who have spent many years studying and translating the Pali suttas into English don't doubt it. Mr. and Mrs. Rhys Davids in their translation of *Dialogues of the Buddha* maintain that when the Pali canon was finally written down the legendary material was still so unsettled that "it was not only possible, it was considered quite the proper thing to *add to or alter it.*" [emphasis added]. In their introduction to *Vinaya Texts*, translators T.W. Rhys Davids and Hermann Oldenberg show an unusual forthrightness when they declare that "there is little doubt" that most of the narratives concerning the Buddha were "mere inventions," although elsewhere Rhys Davids is careful to point out that "the doctrinal material stands on a different footing."[54] Foucher in his gracefully written *The Life of the Buddha* echoes the contentions of Oldenberg and Davids.[55]

While Oldenberg, Foucher, the Rhys Davids, and other respected Buddhist scholars of another generation regard portions of the Pali texts as suspect, contemporary Buddhologists like Edward Conze go even further. In his *Thirty Years of Buddhist Studies* Conze reminds us that the Buddha spoke not Pali but a dialect called Magadhi, and that all his sayings, like those of Jesus, are lost in their original form. He notes that no less than eighteen different schools functioned in the first period of Buddhist history, each with its own scriptures and claims to authority, and argues persuasively that it was an accident of historical transmission more than anything else that accounts for the Theravadin scriptures alone reaching us intact and in their entirety. He goes on to quote Professor Waldschmidt:

> . . .it is not infrequently the Sanskrit, i.e., Mahayana *Mahaparinirvana sutra*, which has probably preserved the original tradition more faithfully, and it has at the least the same value as the Pali text. . .[56]

The scholar Hofinger then adds:

> . . .once again the Pali Canon has come down from the pedestal on which it has stood for so long; it has no more value than the Chinese and Tibetan canonical documents, and occasionally it is even somewhat inferior to them.

That portions of the Pali and Sanskrit scriptures were deliberately altered or omitted to conform to the prejudices or points of view of monk scribes must also not be overlooked. Conze gives this example: In the *Dighanikaya XVI*, the Buddha's last words appear as "Doomed to extinction are composite things; exert yourselves in wakefulness!" But in the Mahaparinirvana sutra there appears only "Doomed to extinction are all composite things." A. Fernandez in an unpublished paper on women in Buddhism points out that where the Sanskrit of the Lotus sutra reads "An enlightened self opened his eyes to the truth without looking to his master for help," the Chinese version says, ". . .he listened to the Buddha's law and accepted it as being true." She then quotes the Japanese scholar Nakamura as saying that this is an example of Chinese monks deliberately modifying a meaning to suit their purpose.

Regarding the question of what the Buddha actually said, then, the conclusion is inescapable: historical facts are beyond our reach, leaving us with only the different versions of Buddhist legend to evaluate. Mrs. Rhys Davids wrapped it up neatly when she observed:

> When believers in the East and historians in the West will come out of the traditional attitude... when we shall no more read, "The Buddha laid down this and denied that," but "the Buddhist church did so"—then we shall at last be fit to try to pull down superstructure and seek for the man...[57]

We can now see, by the way, why Zen is known as a transmission outside the sutras, without reliance on words and letters, and why it does not base itself on any one sutra as do other sects. What this means is that for Zen, truth must be grasped directly and not taken on the authority of the sutras, much less on lifeless intellectual formulas. Not the sutras but the spirit of compassion and reverence informing them; not the words but the realization of the formless reality behind them; not the life of the Buddha but his awakening—this is the stuff of Zen. Zen does not repudiate the sutras—it merely seeks to grasp the Source in which they are grounded, namely, True-mind.

Ultimately the case for shunning animal flesh does not rest on what the Buddha allegedly said or didn't say. What it does rest on is our innate moral goodness, compassion, and pity which, when liberated, lead us to value all forms of life. It is obvious, then, that wilfully to take life, or through the eating of meat indirectly to cause others to kill, runs counter to the deepest instincts of human beings.

MEAT EATING AS A FAMILY ISSUE

To be sure, it is not easy to give up lifetime habits of meat eating. Starting when their children are young, most parents push upon them flesh foods in the honest belief that "Unless you eat your beef and chicken, Johnny, you won't grow up to be big and strong." Under this prodding, even children with a natural aversion to flesh foods are coerced into yielding, and eventually their finer sensibilities are blunted. When they grow older the meat industry's propaganda takes over. Finally meat-eating doctors, themselves unwilling to forego their T-bone steaks, put the last nail into the coffin of vegetarianism by hammering away at the theme that "Meat, fish, and chicken are the best sources of protein"—a demonstrably false statement (see Supplement 1).

Many parents, taking the doctors' dictum as holy writ, go into minor shock when their teenage child suddenly pushes away the meat dish at dinner and quietly announces, "I'm not eating this stuff any more." "Why not?" asks Dad, his face reddening as he manages a grin that scarcely conceals the scorn behind his question, while Mother rolls her eyes toward the ceiling, hands in prayer. And when Tom or Jane answers, more with fact than tact, "Because my stomach is not a dump for scorched animal corpses," the battle lines are drawn. Some parents, especially mothers, are perceptive enough to see such behavior in their son or daughter as a resurgence of long dormant feelings of pity for animals, and are sympathetic. But most parents view it either as an aberration not to be indulged, as a challenge to their authority, as in indictment of their own meat eating, or all three. So they warn, "As long as you're living in our house you've got to eat the way normal people eat. If you want to ruin your health that's your business, but you're not going to do it here." Matters are not improved by psychologists who come up with the facile diagnosis: "Your child is using food as a weapon to emancipate himself from your authority. Don't inflate his self-importance by making an issue of his vegetarianism—it will pass."

For some adolescents vegetarianism is undoubtedly a vehicle of rebellion or a ploy to gain concessions from beleaguered parents. But my own experience with young people convinces me that in most cases their refusal to eat animal flesh is motivated by something deeper and finer: an idealistic desire to do something about pain and suffering—their own as well as others', human and non-human. Avoiding flesh food is the first easily-realized step in that direction. Not all parents, though, regard their child's renunciation of flesh foods with hostility or dismay. One mother told me, "Up to the time my son was twenty my husband and I taught him whatever we could. Now he is teaching us. By his refusal to eat flesh foods he made us see the moral implications of meat eating, and we are grateful to him."

Difficult as it is to turn away from ingrained eating habits, we need to make the effort to achieve a humane diet, for our own sake as well as that of others. Those who have given up meat eating out of pity for sentient beings need not be told what a wonderful feeling it is knowing that no animal has to be sacrificed to provide them with food. Indeed it can be said that until one has ceased eating animals "a part of one's soul remains unawakened," to paraphrase Anatole France. To give the body's chemistry time to adjust to the change in diet, it is best to dispense first with meat, next poultry, and eventually fish. As one's zazen or meditation matures, these foods eventually give one up and it becomes virtually impossible to eat coarse flesh foods.

BUDDHIST PRIESTS AND THE FIRST PRECEPT

Although one can sympathize with lay persons trying to break their attachment to a diet featuring meat, it is something else again to extend those sympathies to monks, priests, and teachers. What business have these latter to propound the Dharma when they possess neither the perception nor compassion to see the connection between meat eating and the killing of harmless animals, and when they lack the self-discipline to put Buddhist compassion before the pleasures of their palates? What right have they to wear the Buddha's robes when they won't or can't honor the bodhisattvic[58] vows they recite daily to liberate all beings?

Buddhism, though still new in the West, has gained many adherents disillusioned with the Western religions on the one hand and attracted to Buddhism's promise of inner peace, wisdom, and compassion on the other. At this point in Buddhist history the West is an oyster whose pearl is ready for the picking, but if the monks and teachers prefer the fish to the pearl they won't touch the hearts of the people and will lose a golden opportunity.

Regrettably, Asian teachers have brought with them to the West many of the cultural prejudices and debased practices that have grown up around Buddhism in their native lands. In many Buddhist centers run by Tibetans, Japanese, Koreans, and monks from Southeast Asian countries meat is openly eaten, as though these teachers never heard of the Mahayana sutras. Worse, Western teachers trained in Asia, or in the West by Asians, often ape the dubious practices of their teachers and teach them to their own students. The Dutch writer van de Wetering in his anecdotal book about life in a rural Zen community on the northeast coast of the United States makes repeated reference to meals of sausage, bacon, and turkey spines bought from the local "factory." "Some of the geese from a flock kept by the community," he writes, "were occasionally sent into town to be slaughtered, because the roshi himself 'couldn't do it.' " Concludes the author, obviously reflecting the roshi's feelings, "A butcher accumulates a lot of bad karma...But there's nothing wrong in eating meat off a body which has been clobbered to death by another." In Paris a buffoon of a roshi holds soireés at which he and his students juggle cocktails while munching meat canapes, careful not to spill either on their Buddhist robes, all no doubt to prove how free and liberated they are. One member of the Rochester Center who had lived in a Zen community in California reported that the roshi there had literally forced some of his students to eat flesh foods to "break them of their attachment to vegetarianism." One can only ask, "What kind of mentality lies behind such bizarre actions?"

In the Asian Buddhist countries the Buddha's Dharma has been steadily eroding. The reasons are many and complex, but certainly the ethics and behavior of the "guardians" of the Dharma have played a large part in this erosion. "How morally slack are the priests of Japan today, how weak their faith in the Buddha's teachings"—this dirge my teacher Yasutani-roshi chanted over and over."What these priests excel in," he would add, "is the ability to cleverly rationalize their defiling of the precepts."

WHALE KILLING AND JAPANESE BUDDHISM

The decay of Japanese Buddhism lamented by Yasutani-roshi may be sensed in an extraordinary memorial service that recently took place in a Zen temple in Japan. Attended by government officials and executives and employees of one of Japan's largest corporations, the event was also witnessed by a sympathetic reporter for *The Baltimore Sun*, who wrote the following account of his experience:

> The Zen temple was large, opulently appointed and evidently prosperous. The occasion was a memorial rite to pray for the souls of the 15,000 who gave their lives in service to the Japanese people during the previous three years.
>
> The mourners were seated according to their rank in the company for which most of them worked. Twenty of them, male executives and government officials dressed in suits and ties, oc-

cupied benches on a raised platform close to the altar. The other 180 persons, mostly jacketless men but including a cluster of young women, sat crosslegged on straw mats to either side of the platform.

Entering to the sounding of a gong, the priests filed in and faced the altar. A big drum sounded. One of the men in business suits stood and welcomed the congregation.

The chief priest, wearing a canary-yellow robe and with his head shaved, began praying: "Release their souls from agony. Let them go over to the Other Side and become Buddhas." Then he and the other priests chanted, on and on, hypnotically, one of the sutras.

When the chanting had ended, the mourners proceeded two-by-two to the altar to light sticks of incense.

Finally the chief priest delivered a short homily: "I am pleased that you have chosen our temple for this service. I used to eat whale meat in the army. And so I feel very close to whales."

The reference to whales wasn't at all out of place, since this service was attended by employees of Japan's largest whaling company. The 15,000 souls they prayed for were those of the whales they had killed.[59]

The reporter then goes on to portray the whalers as distressed and bewildered by criticisms from abroad, particularly the United States, "that they are heartless and cruel sorts who are unnecessarily taking the lives of some of nature's noblest creatures." He quotes the captain of a catcher boat as saying he recalls that it was "the American Occupation authorities who right after World War II instructed that factory ship fleets be sent out to help keep the defeated country from starvation; and while the Japanese are not starving now their per capita consumption of animal protein is less than half that of Americans, and whale meat is an ingredient of school lunches." A retired harpoon gunner told the reporter, "I don't understand the argument of the anti-whaling people. It is the same if you have to kill a cow or chicken to eat—even a fish. If whales were like pigs or cows, making lots of noise before they die, I could never shoot them. Whales die without making noise. They're like fish."[60] The writer then concludes his article with this comment: "Their sensitivities [the harpoon gunners'] would surprise some anti-whaling activists. Inai, for example, killed more than 7,000 whales in 24 years as a gunner. But he said he once saw a fast-swimming

RICHARD ELLIS

mother whale returning to the scene of danger to dive under her slow-moving calf and carry it off. He was so moved by the scene, he said, that he couldn't shoot."

At first blush the service in the temple seems to have the redeeming feature of the "pretense at an apology" to the slaughtered whales, the "homage of a tear." In point of fact, however, this scenario is fatally flawed, and this is why: The first precept of not killing forbids, as we know, the deliberate taking of life; consequently, fishing either as a sport or an occupation is prohibited to Buddhists (slaughters, hunters, and trappers are in the same boat as the fishermen). For a whaling company therefore to enlist the services of Buddhist priests and a Buddhist temple to impart an air of religious sanctity to a Buddhistically improper enterprise—for its employees to pray to Buddha to dispel the agony of the "souls" of the whales they have killed while flouting the Buddha's teachings—this is on a par with the case of the boy who murdered both his parents and then pleaded for clemency on the ground that he was an orphan.

Dr. D.T. Suzuki, the well-known Buddhist philosopher, would agree. In his booklet *The Chain of Compassion* he decries the hypocrisy of those who needlessly take life and then hold Buddhist memorial services for the creatures they have callously slain. He writes:

Buddhists chant sutras and offer incense after these creatures are gone and they say they have thus pacified the spirits of the animals they have killed. They decide that in this way they have nicely put an end to the matter. But can we really dismiss the matter in this manner?. . . Love or compassion is at work in the heart of everything throughout the universe. Why does only man utilize his so-called knowledge to satisfy his selfish passions and then attempt to justify his doings in various hypocritical ways?. . . Buddhists must strive to teach respect and compassion for all creation—compassion is the foundation of their religion. . . [61]

Had the service in the temple been an act of genuine Buddhist piety and not a sham, the whalers and company officials would have repented of their innumerable violations of the first Buddhist precept of not killing; they would have prayed to Kannon, the bodhisattva of compassion, for forgiveness; and they would have pledged to cease the further slaughter of innocent whales. But of course none of this took place. As for the Buddhist priests who lent themselves and their temple to this charade, motivated no doubt by visions of a large donation from the whaling company, their actions speak eloquently of the fallen state of Japanese Buddhism today.

In the years right after World War II Japan was undeniably a poor and hungry country and she may have been justified then in her unrestricted killing of whales for food; that is undoubtedly why the American Occupation authorities encouraged whaling activities. Today, however, when Japan is one of the wealthier countries in the world, with a gross national product second only to that of the United States among the free nations, no such justification exists.

More to the point, however, is the fact that whale meat does not have a significant place in the diet of the Japanese, contrary to what the writer of the article implies. It has been estimated that the Japanese get as little as .3 per cent of their protein from whale meat.[62] Even when I was living in Japan right after World War II and in the early fifties, only the very poor ate the cheap *kujira*, whale meat. Most Japanese didn't like its oily taste and therefore wouldn't eat it. With the benefits of the Japanese "economic miracle" filtering down to rank and file Japanese workers, who are now among the most highly paid in the world, it is safe to assume they are titillating their taste buds with more delectable meat than *kujira*. In fact, the consumption of meat products by the Japanese has risen so dramatically that some say it now ranks second to that of the United States.[63] The lamentable truth is that the Japanese today, and the Soviets too, are slaughtering whales largely for shoe polish, face creams, fertilizer, pet food, and machine lubricants, all of which can be obtained from other sources, in an appalling display of insensitivity to world opinion.[64]

It is not defending the large quantities of animal protein that Americans consume, or justifying the killing of pigs, cows, and chickens from which this protein is mainly obtained, to point out that these animals are not endangered species. Whales are. It is common knowledge that whales are highly intelligent mammals—certainly they are less aggressive and predatory than humans. Moreover, the whalers themselves admit that whales in their concern for their young are almost human. How then can

the Japanese whalers say they are like other fish? More significant in this context than even the intelligence of whales is their
well-developed nervous systems and thus their capacity for suffering great pain. Imagine what it's like to have a harpoon ex-
plode in your insides! Consider in this context the statement of
Dr. H.R. Lillie, a physician who worked with the British whaling
fleet in the Southern Ocean: "The method still used in killing
whales today is antiquated and horrible. . . In one extreme case
that I witnessed, five hours and nine harpoons were required to
kill a female Blue Whale in advanced pregnancy."[65]

Or picture what it's like for a dolphin to be clubbed to death,
a brutal practice engaged in by Japanese fishermen. Recent news
photos have shown Japanese fishermen slaughtering these high-
spirited animals by the thousands in this fashion and machine-
shredding their carcasses, again not for human consumption but
for animal feed and fertilizer. What makes the wholesale destruction of dolphins particularly odious is the universal knowledge
that these remarkable animals and man have always had a
unique relationship. Throughout the ages tales have been told of
the kindness of dolphins to human beings in distress. Jacques
Cousteau documented how dolphins in Mauritania, Africa, would
actually bring fish to the people, and naturalist Tom Garrett has
told of Amazon tribes which cultivate the friendship of dolphins
to protect them against piranha fish and other dangers.[66] The
stories, songs, and legends of peoples of diverse cultures have
celebrated the "high spirits and high virtue" of these singular
creatures. Aristotle wrote that "this creature is remarkable for
the strength of its parental affection." The Greek poet Oppian
pronounced an anathema on dolphin killers in these words:

> Hunting of dolphins is abomination. A man
> Who wilfully brings about their death,
> Can approach the gods no more. They will
> Not love him for his offerings. His touch
> Pollutes their altars, and he defiles all
> Those who live below his roof. As much
> As they loathe the murdering of men
> Do the gods loathe to have death's doom
> Brought on these chieftains of the deep.[67]

HUMAN BEINGS DISTINGUISHED FROM ANIMALS

Meat eaters often argue that in devouring other creatures man, also an animal, is only doing what animals in the wild themselves do, that the survival of one creature demands the death of another. What this argument ignores is that carnivores can survive only by eating other animals—they have no choice their stomachs compel them to—but human beings can survive, and survive well, without devouring other creatures. That man is a predator, and the deadliest of all, no unprejudiced person will deny, for to the extent that he destroys his own kind and other species—the latter as much for sport and profit as for food—no other creature is his equal. Even so, human beings are distinguished from other animals by their powers of reasoning and self-transcendence, their sense of justice and compassion. We pride ourselves on our uniquely human ability to make ethical judgments and take moral responsibility for our actions. To protect the weak and gentle from the homicidal aggressions of the strong and ruthless, we establish laws decreeing that one who wantonly murders another (except in self-defense or in defense of his country) be severely punished for his evil deed, and this often involves the sacrifice of his own life. In our human relationships we disavow, or like to believe we disavow, the morality of might makes right. But where non-humans are concerned, especially those whose flesh or skins we covet, or on whose bodies we wish to conduct lethal experiments, we oppress and exploit them freely, justifying our harsh treatment on the ground that since they are beings of inferior intelligence, with no sense of right and wrong, they have no rights. If the value of a life, human or non-human, is to be judged by the quality of that being's intelligence, then, like the Nazis, we ought to put to death senile and mentally retarded human beings, for many animals are more intelligent and better able to interact with their own species than, say, a mentally retarded adult. Analogously, suppose extraterrestrial beings of a higher intelligence than ours were to invade our planet. Would they be morally justified in destroying and eating us simply because we did not measure up to their levels of intelligence and they liked the taste of our flesh?

From an ethical standpoint, however, the criterion is not a being's intelligence or its ability to make moral judgments but its capacity for suffering pain, physical and emotional. And animals do experience pain—they are not things. They can be lonely, sad, and frightened; they suffer greatly when deprived of their young; and they cling to life as much as human beings do. It is idle to speak, as some do, of destroying livestock painlessly, for there will always be the terror and anguish they experience in the slaughterhouse and in the cattle trucks on the way to their execution, not to mention branding, dehorning, and castration, the most common cruelties they undergo in their rearing for slaughter. Let us ask ourselves, Would we consent to being killed, while in good physical and mental health, just because it could be done painlessly? Do we, ultimately, have the right to deprive other species of their lives when no greater social good is being served, and where compassion does not demand it? How dare we pretend to love justice when for the pleasures of our tongues and palates we murder hundreds of thousands of defenseless animals in cold blood every day without a "shadow of remorse" and without anyone suffering the slightest punishment. What an evil karma we human beings continue to store up for ourselves, what a legacy of violence and terror we bequeath future generations!

EATING ANIMALS WHILE "LOVING" THEM

Ironically, we don't eat the carnivorous beasts, as Rousseau observes, but take them as our model. Even professed animal lovers are not averse to eating their four-legged or feathered friends. The famous ethologist Konrad Lorenz tells us that since childhood he has loved animals and has surrounded himself with many different kinds. Yet on the very first page of the introduction to his book *Man Meets Dog* he confesses:

> Today for breakfast I ate some fried bread and sausage. Both the sausage and the lard that the bread was fried in came from a pig that I used to know as a dear little piglet. Once that stage was over, to save my conscience from conflict I meticulously avoided any further acquaintance with that pig. I should probably only eat animals up to the mental level of fish or, at the most, frogs if I were obliged to kill them myself. It is, of course, hypocritical to avoid, in this way, the moral responsibility for the murder . . . . [68]

How does he justify his avoidance of moral responsibility for what he righly calls murder?

Another feature which exculpates man to some extent is the fact that he is bound by no agreement, by no contract with the animals in question, to treat them as anything but enemies which he has taken prisoner.

One can imagine the animals saying, "With such friends who needs enemies?"

THE KILLING AND EATING
OF ANIMALS BY NATIVE PEOPLES

In spite of the foregoing, the killing and eating of animals may be condoned under certain circumstances. Native peoples like Eskimos and Laplanders presumably have little choice but to hunt and fish in order to preserve a way of life in harmony with their unique environments. What saves them, or at least those still rooted in their traditions, from the karmic fate of the usual hunters and fishermen is their view of hunting and fishing as a holy rite. Since they do not separate themselves from the hunted by feelings of superiority and dominance, their identification with the animals they hunt and fish is grounded in respect for and humility toward the common Life Force that animates and binds them both.[69]

IS KILLING A VEGETABLE
THE SAME AS KILLING AN ANIMAL?

Flesh eaters often say, "If you eat only vegetables you are also taking life. What, then, is the difference between taking the life of, say, a pig and that of a vegetable?" Answer: All the difference in the world. Does a potato cry out when it is taken from the earth the way a calf does when it is taken from its mother? Does a stick of celery scream in pain and terror when it is picked the way a pig does when it is being led to slaughter and is having its throat cut? And how sad, lonely, and frightened can a head of lettuce feel?

We don't need a polygraph to demonstrate that plants have consciousness of a sort, but this consciousness is obviously of a rudimentary kind, far different from that of mammals with well developed nervous systems. Nor do we need tests to prove that cows and pigs and sheep experience pain to the same degree as human beings, for it is common observation that animals wince, howl, wail, and show terror when abused or injured and make every effort to avoid pain.

Actually many fruits and vegetables can be picked without killing or even harming the plants. These include berries, melons, legumes, nuts, seeds, pumpkins, squash, okras, and many other vegetables. Potatoes are taken from the ground after the plant has died. Most vegetables are annuals, harvested at or near the end of their natural life.

In fact there is considerable scientific evidence that our teeth, our jaws, and our long, convoluted intestinal canal are not naturally suited to a flesh diet.[70] The human alimentary canal, for example, is ten or twelve times the length of the body, whereas the digestive tract of carnivores such as the wolf, the lion and the cat is only three times the length of their bodies, enabling them to eliminate rapidly decaying substances like meat in a very short time. Not only this, but because the stomach of a carnivore contains a greater and more powerful quantity of hydrochloric acid than that of a human, it can more easily digest flesh foods. Many scientists now concede that fruits, vegetables, nuts, seeds, and grains appear best suited to the human body.

Finally, we know that we cannot subsist for long without food, and all food is matter that was once alive. But since we *can* subsist well and even thrive without meat, why take animal life in addition to the plant life we need to survive?

Among pseudo Buddhists one will often hear another kind of argument that is as bald-faced as it is specious: "Sure, we eat meat," they say, "what of it? In Buddhism what is most important is not what enters the stomach but what comes out of the mind." Although it is true that ridding oneself of one's delusions, breaking out of the prison of the ego-I into a life of sympathy with all sentient beings is paramount, how can we establish a sympathetic rapport with non-humans while we are feasting on them?

HITLER—
VEGETARIANISM'S SKELETON IN THE CLOSET

The avoidance of flesh foods enjoined by the Mahayana scriptures, it should also be pointed out, is not to be equated with a vegetarianism adopted for purely health reasons. A case in point is Adolph Hitler, the skeleton in the closet of vegetarians. He is said to have given up meat out of a fear of developing cancer.[71] Meat eaters love to cite Hitler's fondness for vegetables as proof that one may eschew meat and still be aggressive, cruel, megalomaniacal, psychopathic, and everything else unlovely. What these critics choose to ignore is that no one has shown that those who tortured and murdered in his name, the S.S. storm troopers and Gestapo, ever shunned meat. The point is that a vegetarianism concerning itself only with one's own health and not the animals'—their pain and suffering—can easily end up as a cultic "ism," an attachment to a particular diet for its own sake. In any case, no one has ever claimed that a meatless diet has the alchemical power to turn base metal into gold.

In the book *Animals, Men and Morals*, a collection of essays subtitled "An enquiry into the maltreatment of non-humans," Patrick Corbett goes to the heart of the matter with these telling words:

> . . . We believe that almost any man if presented with the issue as to whether another living creature should or should not continue to exist, or as to whether it should or should not suffer, would agree, so long as other lives and interests are not at stake, that it *should* live and *should not* suffer. . . . To be generally indifferent to the life and welfare of others while making exceptions in favour of those who happen to be useful to us . . . to be prepared, as were the Nazis, to sacrifice anyone and anything to one's own aggressive impulses: these are to turn one's back upon that model of a . . . loving and respectful life which we all carry with us in our hearts and which . . . we must, if we are truthful, acknowledge in the end.[72]

Isn't it time to stop killing and eating our fellow creatures and begin loving them?

Thus, no creature ever
comes short of its own completeness.
Wherever it stands,
it does not fail to cover the ground.

—Zen Master Dogen

III
SUPPLEMENTS

1/THE PROTEIN ISSUE:
RAISING WAVES WHEN THERE IS NO WIND

UNDOUBTEDLY the most formidable obstacle to many who would dispense with flesh foods is the deep-seated fear that a vegetarian diet will not provide the necessary protein and other nutritional requirements. Such people may be haunted by memories of their grade school science teacher warning that a balanced diet contains members of all the main food groups, including that of "meat and fish." And with only 30 of the nation's 125 medical schools having required courses in nutrition, the words of misinformed doctors often add to one's concern. But with the most recent advances in nutrition research, the popular myth of meat and fish as indispensable protein sources has been stripped of all scientific support, if indeed it ever had any.

How much protein does the body need, anyway? Estimates vary, but among the highest is the Recommended Daily Dietary Allowance (RDA) published by the Food and Nutrition Board of the National Academy of Sciences. ["Protein," observed Carl Pfeiffer, Ph.D., M.D., "is probably one of the few nutritional factors for which the RDA does not underestimate our needs."][1] The Academy's 1973 revised figures are 44-56 grams for adult males, 44-48 grams for adult females (76 gm. during pregnancy, 66 during lactation), and 23-36 grams for children. Bear in mind that there are some 450 grams in a pound.

Dr. Henry Sherman, of Columbia University, after reviewing 109 nitrogen balance studies (the test most often utilized for protein adequacy) spanning 32 years, concluded that 1 gm. protein per kilogram body weight (70 gm. for a 154-pound adult) was sufficient to provide a margin of safety of *50-100 per cent* for adult maintenance (this places the minimum requirement at 35-47 gm.)[2] Evidence of the need for even less protein has been obtained in later studies.

It is illuminating to compare even the relatively high RDA figures for protein need with the protein content measured in non-flesh diets in many experiments. In a 1954 Harvard research project, for instance, even "pure vegetarians" (those who abstain from eggs and dairy products as well as flesh foods) received 83 gm. and 61 gm. (men and women, respectively) protein a day; the lacto-ovo-vegetarians (who eat eggs and dairy products as well) obtained 98 and 82 gm., respectively.[3]

A reason commonly heard for not giving up flesh foods is, "I do heavy work, so I need meat for strength." Although it may be true that strenuous activity requires higher protein consumption, there is no evidence that a vegetarian diet, especially when supplemented with eggs or dairy products, fails to meet even the highest demand for protein. Dr. Russell Chittenden, physiological chemist at Yale University, spent months studying athletes and soldiers on a low protein diet, and found that "44-53 gm. (less than 2 oz.) of protein sufficed to keep them in excellent health, with their physical abilities in no way lessened."[4] In other experiments at Yale University and at Brussels University, vegetarians demonstrated far greater endurance, stamina, and quickness of recovery from fatigue than meat eaters.[5] The Vegetarian Cycling and Athletic Club of Great Britain at one time held as many as 40 per cent of the national cycling records, and the majority of cycling winners all over Europe have been vegetarians.[6] Famous vegetarian swimmers include Murray Rose, triple gold medal winner in the 1956 Olympics, whose non-flesh diet began at age 2, and Bill Pickering, who set a world's record for the fastest crossing of the English Channel. Other vegetarians from all over the world have set records in wrestling, boxing, and cross-country and marathon running.

Although protein is singled out for attention in areas where malnutrition is prevalent, the problem is often fundamentally one of a deficit in total calories. For even when protein is in adequate supply, symptoms of protein deficiency may still appear if the diet provides insufficient calories since, under these circumstances, some of the protein is utilized for energy.

We may conclude with most scientists, then, that it would be difficult to devise a diet in which protein is of insufficient *quantity*, especially since plants generally rank higher than animal products in protein content, or the proportion of useable protein to total weight. But protein *quality* is another vital factor that must be considered.

Protein is a long molecule chain made up of links called amino acids. These amino acids are the "building blocks" of all living organisms, necessary for growth, for the maintenance of tissues and bones, hair and nails, for combating infection and disease, and for certain vital metabolic reactions in the body. Although there are 22 amino acids, only 8 of them (9 in the case of children) cannot be synthesized by the body and so must be obtained from foods. Our bodies need all 8 of these "essential" amino acids simultaneously and in the correct proportion. A "complete" protein is one which meets these requirements when isolated and fed as the only protein in the diet—conditions that would be obtained only in a laboratory, since any ordinary diet contains many kinds of proteins of various compositions.

Eggs, milk, and cheese, like meat, each contain all the essential amino acids; in fact, each of them surpasses meat in protein value.[7] Accordingly, a diet that includes eggs and/or dairy products indisputably provides a rich supply of highest quality protein. But even these unique "complete" protein foods may be dispensed with since the adequacy of protein intake depends, not on the completeness of any single protein food, but on the composition of the mixture of amino acids present in all the proteins of the meal. By combining two plant foods, neither of which is individually complete, amino acid patterns can be made to complement or balance, each other to form a complete, high-quality protein. For example, the amino acids in short supply in rice are plentiful in legumes and vice versa, so that rice eaten with legumes becomes a complete protein. Thus meals of plant foods can be planned that far exceed meat in protein value.

In 1964 two researchers with the Institute of Nutrition of Central America and Panama declared at the Sixth International Congress of Nutrition:

> From a nutritional point of view animal or vegetable proteins should not be differentiated. It is known today that the relative

concentration of the amino acids, particularly of the essential ones, is the most important factor determining the biological value of a protein.... By combining different proteins in appropriate ways, vegetable proteins cannot be distinguished nutritionally from those of animal origin. The amino acids and not the proteins should be considered as the nutritional units.[8]

Further confirmation of this breakthrough in nutritional understanding appeared in *Samson Wright's Applied Physiology*:

In any mixed diet, even if wholly of plant origin, the proteins are sure to be sufficiently varied to compensate for any individual inadequacies in amino acid content, if only the total amount of protein is sufficient.[9]

It requires no great exertion or imagination to maintain a non-flesh diet in which the amino acid deficiency of one food is supplemented by the amino acid contained in others. In fact, the traditional diets of most cultures naturally yield mutually complementing amino acid patterns. Many native peoples of the Americas, for instance, have subsisted for generations on corn and beans as well as rice and beans, both complete protein combinations. Similarly, the staple long found in India is rice and *dahl* (beans and peas), also a complete protein. In Japan, essentially a vegetarian country until the mid-19th century, the traditional combination was and still is rice with soybean products. A group of Buddhist monks in Japan whose pure plant diet consisted chiefly of rice and barley, with soy products, vegetables, and rapeseed oil, were shown in a study to be in good health.[10] China has also relied heavily on rice and beans, and the millet-corn-soybean mixture which is the staple of North China peasants has been reported to be of sound protein value.

Many other native peoples have flourished for centuries without the least concern about "getting enough protein." Dr. S.A. Riaz, of the Glasgow Royal Infirmary, marveled at the people he visited living at altitudes of 8,000-12,000 feet in the valley of Kaghan, Gilzit, Hunza, and other mountainous areas of northwest Pakistan:

Consuming the simplest possible diets of wheat, corn, potatoes, onions, and fruits, they trudge up and down the rough mountain paths for anything up to fifty miles a day. They have existed thus for perhaps many thousands of years.... Their remarkable physical fitness, absence of obesity, caries-free teeth, and longevity are always cited.[11]

The United States is not without its own traditional complete combinations from non-flesh sources. In *Chemistry of Food and Nutrition* (1962), Dr. Henry Sherman, of Columbia University, cited a well-known grain-legume combination: "The customary combination of baked beans and brown bread makes a 'main dish' that ranks with meat as a source of nutritionally good protein and vitamins of the B group." Other all-American complete protein combinations are peanut butter sandwiches (grain-nuts), cheese sandwiches (grain-dairy), and a bowl of breakfast cereal (cereal grain-milk).

Certainly there are all too many underprivileged areas of the world plagued by nutritional diseases. But as nutrition authorities U.D. Register, Ph.D., R.D., and L.M. Sonnenberg, R.D., pointed out at the 55th Annual Meeting of the American Dietetic Association in 1972, referring to the reports of such diseases:

> These generally show that the diseases are due, not to a vegetarian diet as such, but to a gross shortage of food, or to a diet consisting largely of such foods as refined cornmeal, cassava root, tapioca, or white rice, with practically no milk, eggs, leafy vegetables, legumes, or fruits.[12]

The excessive use of protein-free calories is a problem by no means limited to underdeveloped countries. It has been estimated that 65 per cent of calories in the typical American diet are from sugars, fats, and oils.[13] While unrefined foods with few exceptions supply ample protein, sugars, fats, and oils contain no protein. This means that as these "empty" calories increase in dietary proportion, as in the industrialized nations, the remaining calories must assume an ever-greater burden of providing adequate protein. Vegetarians who eat no eggs or dairy products, then, should be especially careful not to dilute protein and other nutrients with empty calories.

Not only normal adults but pregnant women, adolescents, and children have all been declared on safe ground with a meatless diet. An analysis of the protein intake in an oft-quoted study of vegetarian (both lacto-ovo- and pure) and nonvegetarian adult men and women, pregnant women, and adolescents conducted by Dr. Mervyn Hardinge, M.D., Dr. P.H., Ph.D., of the

Loma Linda University School of Medicine, and Frederick Stare, M.D., Ph.D., of the Harvard University School of Public Health, revealed that, after allowing for the higher protein needs of the pregnant women and adolescents, every group, including the pure vegetarians, met and exceeded twice its minimum requirements of essential amino acids.[14]

For parents concerned that their growing children will not receive ample protein without eating flesh, the literature also offers reassurance. Sir Stanley Davidson in *Human Nutrition and Dietetics* reports, for example, "It is now known that suitable mixtures of vegetable proteins can replace satisfactorily the animal protein in the diet of the young child."

An editorial that appeared in *Lancet*, the highly respected British medical journal, dismissed the long-rumored superiority of flesh protein in these words:

> Formerly vegetable proteins were classified as second-class and regarded as inferior to first-class proteins of animal origin; but this distinction has now been generally discarded. Certainly some vegetable proteins, if fed as the sole source of protein, are of relatively low value for promoting growth; but many field trials have shown that the proteins provided by suitable mixtures of vegetable origin enable children to grow no less well than children provided with milk and other animal proteins. Widdowson and McCance's work in German orphanages showed that children could grow well and remain in excellent health without milk, provided they received a diet containing a good mixture of vegetable proteins.[15]

Cautionary advice: Although plants are generally far richer in vitamins and minerals than are meat and fish, two nutrients that may easily be lacking in the non-flesh diet and thus warrant the attention of vegetarians are vitamin B_{12} and zinc. Except in negligible quantities, vitamin B_{12} is found only in animal products, so that whereas a lacto-ovo-vegetarian need have no concern about it, the pure vegetarian should either take nutritional yeast or B_{12} tablets. According to Dr. Pfeiffer (previously quoted), the worst danger of zinc insufficiency is that the average vegetarian may consume large quantities of beans, legumes, and grains, foods rich in phytates, which bind zinc in the digestive system. But the process of fermentation (thus baker's yeast) and sprouts neutralize phytates. If one eats eggs, milk, wheat bran, wheat germ, pumpkin seeds, sunflower seeds, or nuts, the sources richest in zinc, a tablet supplement may not be necessary.

2/MEAT IS NO TREAT:
THE HAZARDS OF EATING ANIMAL FLESH

The health hazards of eating meat are legion. For example, world health statistics consistently show short life expectancies among heavy flesh-eating peoples. Eskimos, Laplanders, Greenlanders, and Russian Kurgis tribes, who all live on high animal protein diets, have the lowest life expectancies in the world— 30-40 years—while Bulgarians, Russian Caucasians, Yucatan Indians, East Indian Todas, and the Hunzakuts, in Pakistan, all of whom subsist on low protein diets, have life expectancies of 90-100 years. Americans, the heaviest meat eaters in the world, are in twenty-first place in life expectancy among *industrialized* nations.[16]

During World War I a land and sea blockade of Denmark forced that country to adopt a 1-year rationing program that virtually eliminated meat from the diet of its people. To the amazement of the authorities, statistics at the end of the year showed improved health and a mortality rate lowered 17 per cent. Norway's similar rationing program in World War II yielded the same results, with a drop in deaths from circulatory diseases in particular. Significantly, the mortality rates of both countries rebounded to pre-war levels after the rationing programs had ended and meat had been reinstated in the diet.

Cancer is probably the disease most often correlated in scientific studies with a high-meat diet. Reporting on cancer of the colon in the *Journal of the National Cancer Institute*, Drs. Bandaru Reddy and Ernest Wynder stated, "Populations in high risk areas consume diets high in animal protein and fat; people in low risk areas eat food low in such components but high in vegetable protein and fiber."[17] Dr. John W. Berg wrote in *The Wall Street Journal* (Oct. 25, 1973): "There is now substantial evidence that beef consumption is a key factor in determining bowel cancer."

Meat, with its high content of saturated fat or cholesterol, is considered by many researchers as the leading cause of heart disease. Studies have found lower levels of both cholesterol and blood pressure in vegetarians than in non-vegetarians. The *Journal of the American Medical Association* has reported, "...a vegetarian diet can prevent 90 per cent of our thrombo-embolic disease and 94 per cent of our coronary occlusions."[18]

Meat consumption has been widely implicated as contributing not only to the chronic and the degenerative diseases, but to acute diseases and infections as well. Why? First of all, slaughter terminates the normal cleansing functions of the body and leaves the animal saturated with its own waste substances. *The Encyclopaedia Britannica* touches briefly on some of these "extras" available to the meat eater: "Toxic wastes, including uric acid, are present in the blood and tissue, as also are dead and virulent bacteria, not only from the putrefactory process, but from animal diseases, such as hoof and mouth disease, contagious abortion, swine fever, malignant tumors, etc."[19] The uric acid deposits in the muscle fibers of meats are too much for one's kidneys and liver to eliminate in addition to the body's own daily production of uric acid, and the excess can cause gout, rheumatism, headache, epilepsy, hardening of the arteries and nervousness. Uric acid that has become putrified produces an effect similar to caffeine, so that a higher level of restlessness, anxiety, and aggressiveness is usually the result of eating meat over a long time. Uric acid putrefaction also causes body odor.

Slaughter also initiates the rapid process of decomposition, putting the meat packers, transporters, and retailers in a race all too often lost to spoilage. Meat putrifies more readily than any other food, since animal flesh is dead matter, and unless refrigerated or preserved it decays immediately. Frankfurters, hamburgers, and other ground meats are particularly susceptible to putrefaction for the reason that grinding breaks down tissues and releases cell fluids that provide a hospitable breeding ground for bacteria. *Consumer Reports* stated in an August, 1971, survey of hamburger that 20 per cent of the 126 ready-ground samples it analyzed had begun to spoil. In its study of frankfurters, released in February, 1972, the same was reported of more than 40 per cent of the samples.

But long before putrefaction and bodily waste deposits can do their damage the artificial poisoning of meat begins. In 1979 the General Accounting Office (the congressional audit agency) issued a report of a study showing that "Of the 143 drugs and pesticides GAO identified as likely to leave residues in raw poultry and meat, 42 are suspected of causing cancer, 20 of causing birth defects, and 6 of causing mutations."[20] The chain of burgeoning toxicity begins in the fields of grain, which are full of artificial pesticides and fertilizers that when transferred through the food chain can acquire deadly potency. Frances Lappé in her acclaimed *Diet for a Small Planet* elaborates as follows: "Thus, as big fish eat smaller fish, or as cows eat grass (or feed), whatever pesticides they eat are largely retained and passed on. So if man is eating at the 'top' of such food chains, he becomes the final consumer and thus the recipient of the highest concentration of pesticide residues."[21]

Although in the United States the use of DDT in pesticides has now been banned, in Mexico it is still legal, so that livestock imported from there may have been fattened on feed laced with it. Since DDT accumulates in an animal for the 15 months or so it is being raised, it is estimated that DDT-infected meat contains thirteen times the concentration of DDT found in similarly tainted vegetables, fruits, and grains.[22]

Diethylstilbestrol (DES, or "stilbestrol"), a powerful synthetic sex hormone which when mixed into feed or implanted directly stimulates growth while decreasing food consumption, was finally declared illegal in the U.S. (after thirty-six other countries had done so) in 1979 because of strong evidence linking it to cancer and sterility in humans. Yet almost a year after its ban, a far-reaching investigation by the U.S. Food and Drug Administration (FDA) and U.S. Agriculture Department revealed that as many as 200,000 head of cattle were involved in nation-wide illegal DES operations.[23] Furthermore, the drug is still legally used on livestock from Mexico that are subsequently shipped into the U.S.

Even with DES having fallen from grace, livestock breeders in this country face no shortage of growth-promoting chemicals for their herds. Those now used include melengestrol acetate (MGA, which provides a 6 per cent weight gain over DES), zeranol, progesterone, testosterone propionate, furazolidone,

3-nitro-4-hydroxyphenyl arsenic acid, sodium arsanilate, and tylosin phosphate. Arsenic, another notorious carcinogen, is stirred into the feed of meat animals in the form of arsenic compounds, used again as growth stimulants. It is also the main component of chemical solutions into which cattle are "dipped" to rid them of mites, ticks, and other parasites.

Currently it is antibiotics that are generating more widespread concern than any other additive used in the meat industry. According to the Office of Technology Assessment (the scientific research arm of Congress), almost all livestock in the U.S. receive, in addition to antibiotics given therapeutically and regular vaccinations, some kind of antibiotics in their feed on a continual basis. Why? Partly because livestock breeders discovered decades ago that supplementing feed with low, subtherapeutic levels of antibiotics inexplicably improves weight gain and feed efficiency in farm animals and also because breeders contend that keeping animals on a continuous supply of antibiotics is cheaper than maintaining a certain level of sanitation in the environment. This steady diet of antibiotics eliminates the bacteria still sensitive to them, which are normally in the vast majority, while the resistant bacteria multiply and, say a growing number of scientists, eventually reach the human population through the food chain as well as by contact with farm animals and the environment.

Meanwhile, antibiotic-resistant organisms in humans are proliferating worldwide at an alarming rate. According to a 1980 report, "In the 1960's and '70's thousands of hospitalized Americans and tens of thousands of Central and South Americans died because of antibiotic resistance."[24] Strains of gonorrhea, pneumonia, infantile meningitis, typhoid, and salmonella (food poisoning) all are growing more stubbornly resistant to penicillin and tetracycline—significantly, the two antibiotics most popularly used both in human therapy and animal feed.

Other countries have responded to this growing threat. In 1971 Britain proscribed the supplementing of animal feed with antibiotics that are used in the treatment of human disease, a ban supported by the World Health Organization and later joined in similar measure by Holland, Germany, Czechoslovakia, and the Scandinavian countries. In the United States increasing numbers of scientists, government task forces, and the FDA itself struggle in vain against the pharmaceutical industry to enact similar legislation. Meanwhile doctors switch to more toxic, less efficient drugs in order to bring these resurgent diseases under control.

Despite the profligate use of antibiotics by livestock breeders, a disturbing incidence of cancer and other diseases among animals raised for slaughter continues. According to *The Meat Handbook*, there are over seventy known animal diseases that can be transmitted to man.[25] One government report stated that over 90 per cent of chicken from most of the flocks in this country and abroad are infected with leukosis, or chicken cancer;[26] the poultry processing industry has been listed by the Bureau of Labor as one of the most hazardous occupations due to the dangers of contracting diseases. Moreover, leukosis usually occurs in carrier form, without tumors large enough to be spotted by even the most conscientious inspector. And what if cancers or other signs of disease *are* visible to inspectors? Often, if not usually, the growth is simply cut out and the rest of the carcass that nurtured the malignancy or disease sent through. The *Washington Post* reported on February 10, 1970, that "more than 10 per cent of the 30.1 million cattle carcasses approved by federal inspectors underwent some post-mortem whittling for removal of offending parts." Still, consumers can be grateful when even part of a diseased animal is rejected, for it is not uncommon for carcasses to pass before a meat inspector at the rate of up to 11,000 an hour.[27]

It is also widely acknowledged by experts that livestock breeders will often rush diseased animals to slaughter to avoid having them die first from sickness. "The slaughterhouse is the salvation of the farmer," reports Dr. Richard Walden, an M.D. and veterinarian who worked as a meat inspector. "When he is losing his animals to disease he just ships them off to market and hopes they are accepted. . . . One of the first suggestions a vet is supposed to make is, 'Ship it to market.' "[28] Since of course no blood studies or other laboratory analyses are required before slaughter, diseases not advanced enough to manifest themselves outwardly go undetected—and straight to the supermarket.

Still more poisons go into animals destined for slaughter: tranquilizers such as promazine, reserpine, and zinc bacitracin to enhance their appetites (often they are force-fed) or to increase their milk production through activating the hypothalamus; enzymes that accelerate the "aging" process of the meat of the slaughtered animal; and, just prior to slaughter, sodium pentobarbital, an anesthetic, to delay color changes in their muscles and retain the redness of fresh meat.

After slaughter comes the problem of retarding the decay and putrefaction process. To preserve sandwich and luncheon meats, meat packers utilize sodium nitrate and sodium nitrite, which carry the cosmetic bonus of rendering meat a fresh-looking pink. Sodium nitrite has been shown to combine with chemicals in the human body to form cancer-producing substances called nitrosamines and to deprive the hemoglobin of its oxygen-carrying properties. Dr. Charles Edwards, Commissioner of the FDA, testified to a House Subcommittee in March 1971, that it can also be poisonous to small children, can deform the fetuses of pregnant women, and can severely harm anemic persons.

Sodium sulfite, which destroys vitamin B, is yet another carcinogenic chemical commonly added to meat. It masks the odor of spoiled meat and causes it to retain its "fresh" red color no matter how old or rancid it is.

Finally, investigations of meat processing plants continue to yield horror stories of unsanitary conditions and corrupt and grossly inadequate inspection practices. Federal inspection, required of only those 20 per cent of the country's slaughterhouses which sell meat across state lines, in theory demands higher standards than local and state inspection. Yet in 1968 a health inspector found seventy-five violations in a federally inspected New York kosher sausage plant, reporting:

> The worn gears in the meat grinder were rusty and caked with bits of old fat and meat. Paint was scaling off the equipment and falling into the hot dog mixtures. Fresh meat was being stored in rusty tubs.
>
> A sterilizer required in Federal plants to contain 180-degree water for sterilization of knives that are dropped on the floor was full of cold, greasy water. A dead roach floated in the scum of the water surface.
>
> Evidence of rats was everywhere, even where meat was being handled. And there was a Federal inspector on the premises.[29]

Three years later *Consumer Reports*, in its August, 1971, article on hamburger, examined 250 one-pound samples for
wholesomeness, measuring the count of coliform bacteria, which
usually indicates fecal contamination and the presence of
disease-causing organisms. Only 27 per cent of the samples passed their test, while 52 per cent had coliform counts higher than
ten times their upper limit of wholesomeness.

In 1973 the *New York Times* obtained a copy of the latest
meat plant survey by the U.S. Department of Agriculture's inter-
nal policing agency, the Office of the Inspector General, whose
reports are rarely made public. The survey found "conditions
that could endanger consumer health in 43 per cent of meat and
poultry plants checked."[30] Besides detailing many conditions, the
report cited other widespread problems revealed in a study 3
years earlier that still persisted: inadequate supervision of meat-
import inspections, inadequate training and laxity among inspectors, conflicts of interest, neglect of duty, and falsification of
records.

As one educates oneself to the slovenly "inspection" practices and filthy conditions of meat processing plants, as well as
to the antibiotics, hormones, tranquilizers, pesticides, dyes,
deodorants, radiation, preservatives, stabilizers, plastic residues,
and other harmful substances contained in meat, not to mention
its own bodily poisons, putrefactive properties, and diseases, one
acquires an appreciation of the following story:

> When a woman on a plane was served the vegetarian meal
> she had ordered, she noticed that the man sitting next to her had
> also ordered one. Turning to him she asked, "Pardon me, but are
> you a vegetarian too?"
> "No," he replied, "I'm a meat inspector."

3/MEAT'S BY-PRODUCTS:
HUNGER, WASTE, AND POLLUTION

It is no small comfort to those who abstain from meat to know that they can be well nourished without causing the suffering and death of any animal, and that they are being spared the toxic contaminants with which animal flesh is saturated. But many people, especially those most socially and ecologically aware, find in a vegetarian diet still another great merit: easing the problems of world hunger and waste of natural resources.

Economists and agricultural experts agree that the world food supply is limited, in part, by the gross inefficiency of an animal diet in terms of the return it gives for land used. Plants produce far more protein per acre than do livestock: an acre used for cereals can provide five times as much protein as an acre used for meat production; an acre used for legumes can yield ten times as much. Yet more than half of the harvested agricultural land in the United States is planted with feed crops. According to *The United States and World Resources*, if this land were used instead for the direct production of human food, the total production of food measured in calories would be at least four times as great.[31] Meanwhile, the United Nations' Food and Agriculture Organization (FAO) estimates that 1-1½ billion of the world's people are either hungry or malnourished, including 500 million on the edge of starvation.

The United States Department of Agriculture reported that 91 per cent of the corn, 77 per cent of the soybean meal, 64 per cent of the barley, 88 per cent of the oats, and 99 per cent of the grain sorghum crops used in the United States in 1971 were fed directly to livestock animals. Furthermore, farm animals are now gobbling up high-protein fish meal as well; half the world fish catch of 1968 was fed to livestock instead of people. Finally, the concentrated use of agricultural land in response to ever increasing demands for meat depletes the soil and lowers the quality of non-meat crops, notably grains.

Equally sobering are statistics showing how much plant protein is lost when converted by livestock to meat protein. Livestock require an average eight pounds of plant protein to produce one pound of animal protein, with the conversion ratio for cows the worst: twenty-one to one.[32] Frances Lappé, hunger and agriculture expert with the Institute of Food and Development Policy, estimates that as a result of this tragically inefficient use of plant food for animal feed, every year 118 million tons of plant protein become unavailable to man—an amount equivalent to 90 per cent of the yearly world protein deficit![33] It would appear self-evident that, as the Director General of the United Nations' FAO, Mr. A.H. Boerma, concluded, "If we are to bring about a real improvement in the diet of the neediest, we must aim at a greater intake of vegetable protein."[34]

In the face of such dramatic statistics the following argument may be heard: "But the United States produces such abundant harvests of grain and other plant food that it can keep its own people well-supplied with meat and still have a huge surplus left over for export." Leaving aside the many Americans who remain ill-fed, what is the real effect on global hunger of the much-touted U.S. grain surplus? Half of the United States' agricultural exports end up in the bellies of cows, chickens, sheep, hogs, and other livestock, who drastically reduce it to meat protein that is available to only the relatively small proportion of the world's people—and its best-fed—who can pay for it. Worse yet, the meat consumed in this country includes that of animals fattened on feed grown on foreign soil, often of the world's most impoverished countries. The United States is the world's leading beef importer, importing 40 per cent of all beef in world trade.[35] In 1973 this country imported 2 billion pounds of meat, which, though only 7 per cent of our production, is no insignificant amount to the countries whose great loss of plant protein those cattle represent.

How else does the demand for meat, with its gross waste of plant protein, fit into the larger picture of global hunger? Let us look at some of the countries where malnutrition is most severe and widespread, drawing on information that appears in the book *Food First*, by Frances Lappé and Joseph Collins:

- In Central America and the Dominican Republic from one third to one half of total meat production is exported—principally to the United States. Alan Berg in his Brookings Institution study of world nutrition reported that much of the meat in Central America is "ending up not in Latin American stomachs but in franchised restaurant hamburgers in the United States." [p. 289]
- The best land in Colombia is frequently used for grazing cattle, and most of the country's increased yield of grain as a result of its Green Revolution of the 1960's was fed to livestock. [p. 166] Also in Colombia, a big push for increased poultry production (initiated by a giant U.S. animal feed corporation) convinced many farmers to switch from crops used for people (corn and traditional beans) to the more profitable sorghum and soybeans used strictly for chicken feed; consequently, the country's poorest could afford neither what was formerly their single accessible protein source—the now scarcer and higher-priced corn and traditional beans—*nor* the luxury of its so-called replacement, chicken. [p. 293]
- In the Sahelian countries of Africa, cattle exports during 1971, the first year of the devastating drought, totalled over 200 million pounds, an increase of 41 per cent over 1968. [p. 89] In Mali, one of those countries, the acreage planted in peanuts in 1972 was more than double the amount in 1966. But who got the peanuts? Europe's cattle, mostly.[36]
- Several years ago some enterprising meat producers actually began flying cattle into Haiti for grazing and then re-export to the American meat market.[37]
- On a visit to Haiti, Lappé and Collins reported: "We were particularly struck to see the miserable shacks of the landless along the edge of fertile irrigated fields growing feed for thousands of pigs that wind up as sausages for Chicago's Servbest Foods. Meanwhile the majority of Haitians are left to ravage the once-green mountain slopes in near futile efforts to grow food." [p. 42]

Meat production takes a further toll on resources through commercial ranching and overgrazing of cattle. Although the traditional nomadic grazing of mixed herds is regarded by experts as a way of using marginal land that could not yield crops for direct human consumption anyway, the fenced-in grazing of homogeneous herds can often ruin valuable agricultural land by stripping it bare, a growing phenomenon in the United States that is causing concern among ecologists. Lappé and Collins maintain that commercial ranching in Africa, geared primarily to exporting beef, "looms as a grave threat to Africa's semi-arid lands and their traditional inhabitants. . .[It] would mean expensive, imported inputs with serious environmental risks, the extinction of many species of animals, and increased vulnerability to widely fluctuating foreign beef markets.[38] Yet foreign investors are not to be denied the natural bounty of Africa. *Food First* reports a plan by European corporations to begin numerous ranching projects on cheap yet fertile grazing land in Kenya, the Sudan, and Ethiopia that would draw on Green Revolution grains as cattle feed—cattle, of course, bound eventually for European dinner tables.

The business of meat production lays waste to other earth resources besides food. In *Proteins: Their Chemistry and Politics* Dr. Aaron Altschul estimates the expenditure of water involved in a pure vegetarian diet, taking into consideration crop irrigation and the washing and cooking of the food before eating it, at 300 gallons a day per person; but for the person on an omnivorous diet (flesh foods, plant foods, dairy products, and eggs), with its added expenditure of drinking water for livestock and the water used in the slaughterhouse, the figure is an incredible 2,500 gallons a day. (The lacto-ovo-vegetarian's consumption falls between these two extremes.)[39]

Still another damning feature of a meat diet is the appalling pollution it engenders, beginning in the feedlots. Dr. Harold Bernard, an agricultural expert with the United States Environmental Protection Agency, stated in the Nov. 8, 1971, *Newsweek* that the runoffs of liquid and solid wastes from the millions of animals on the 206,000 feedlots in the United States are "ten to several hundred times more concentrated than raw domestic sewage." Dr. Bernard went on to say, "When the highly concentrated wastes in a runoff flow into a stream or river, the results can be—and frequently are—catastrophic. The amount of dissolved oxygen in the waterway will be sharply reduced, while levels of ammonia, nitrates, phosphates and bacteria soar." Then there is the sewage discharged by slaughterhouses. In a study of meat-packing wastes in Omaha, Nebraska, it was reported that slaughterhouses there spew over 100,000 pounds of grease, carcass dressing, casing cleaning, intestinal waste, paunch manure and fecal matter from the viscera into the sewer system (and from there into the Missouri River) *each day.*[40] It has been estimated that the contribution of livestock to water pollution is more than ten times that of people and more than three times that of industry.[41]

The problem of global hunger is vastly complex, and admittedly no one is without a measure of responsibility for the economic, social, and political conditions that perpetuate famine. Yet this much is certain: so long as there is demand for meat, livestock will continue to fatten on many times the protein they yield, to pollute the earth with their wastes, and in the process to indirectly cause incalculable further pollution and consumption of water. Conversely, by abandoning meat we can help to maximize the earth's potential for nourishing its inhabitants and at the same time minimize the waste and abuse of the resources necessary for that purpose.

4/FOOD FOR THOUGHT:
WHAT NOTABLE PERSONS HAVE SAID ABOUT FLESH EATING

BENTHAM, JEREMY *(1748-1832, English philosopher, economist and jurist)*

The day may come when the rest of the animal creation may acquire those rights which never could have been withholden from them but by the hand of tyranny. . . . It may come one day to be recognized that the number of the legs, the villosity of the skin, or the termination of the *os sacrum* are reasons equally insufficient for abandoning a sensitive being to the same fate. What else is it that should trace the insuperable line? Is it the faculty of reason or, perhaps, the faculty of discourse? But a full-grown horse or dog is beyond comparison a more rational, as well as a more conversable animal, than an infant of a day, or a week, or even a month, old. But suppose the case were otherwise, what would it avail? The question is not, Can they *reason*? nor Can they *talk*? but Can they *suffer*?

(from *The Principles of Morals and Legislation*)

BESANT, ANNIE *(1847-1933, English philosopher, humanitarian and social reformer, active in India's movement for independence)*

[People who eat meat] are responsible for all the pain that grows out of meat-eating, and which is necessitated by the use of sentient animals as food; not only the horrors of the slaughterhouse, but also the preliminary horrors of the railway traffic, of the steamboat and ship traffic; all the starvation and the thirst and the prolonged misery of fear which these unhappy creatures have to pass through for the gratification of the appetite of man. . . . All pain acts as a record against humanity and slackens and retards the whole of human growth. . . .

BUDDHA *(563-483 B.C.)*

For fear of causing terror to living beings...let the Bodhisattva who is disciplining himself to attain compassion refrain from eating flesh.

(from *The Lankavatara sutra*)

DA VINCI, LEONARDO *(1452-1519, Italian painter, sculptor, architect, engineer and scientist)*

Truly man is the king of beasts, for his brutality exceeds theirs. We live by the death of others: We are burial places!

(from Merijkowsky's *Romance of Leonardo da Vinci*)

* * *

I have from an early age abjured the use of meat, and the time will come when men such as I will look upon the murder of animals as they now look upon the murder of men.

(from *da Vinci's Notes*)

DIOGENES *(412?-323? B.C.; Greek philosopher)*

We might as well eat the flesh of men as the flesh of other animals.

EMERSON, RALPH WALDO *(1803-1883, American essayist, philosopher and poet)*

You have just dined; and however scrupulously the slaughterhouse is concealed in a graceful distance of miles, there is complicity.

GANDHI, MOHANDAS *(1869-1948, Hindu nationalist leader and social reformer)*

The greatness of a nation and its moral progress can be judged by the way its animals are treated.

* * *

I do not regard flesh food as necessary for us. I hold flesh food to be unsuited to our species. We err in copying the lower animal world if we are superior to it.

* * *

The only way to live is to let live.

JESUS *(3 A.D.-36 A.D.)*

And the flesh of slain beasts in his body will become his own tomb. For I tell you truly, he who kills, kills himself, and whoso eats the flesh of slain beasts eats the body of death.

(from *The Essene Gospel of Peace*)

KAFKA, FRANZ *(1883-1924, influential Austrian-Czech writer)*

Now I can look at you in peace; I don't eat you any more. (Comment made while admiring fish in an aquarium)

KELLOGG, JOHN HARVEY *(1852-1943, American surgeon, founder of Battle Creek Sanatorium)*

Flesh foods are not the best nourishment for human beings and were not the food of our primitive ancestors. They are secondary or secondhand products, since all food comes originally from the vegetable kindgom. There is nothing necessary or desirable for human nutrition to be found in meats or flesh foods which is not found in and derived from vegetable products. A dead cow or sheep lying in a pasture is recognized as carrion. The same sort of carcass dressed and hung up in a butcher's stall passes as food! Careful microscopic examination may show little or no difference between the fence corner carcass and the butcher shop carcass. Both are swarming with colon germs and redolent with putrefaction.

MAETERLINCK, COUNT MAURICE *(1862-1949, Belgian playwright, essayist and poet)*

Were the belief one day to become general that man could dispense with animal food, there would ensue not only a great economic revolution, but a moral improvement as well.

MILL, JOHN STUART *(1806-1873, English philosopher and economist)*

Granted that any practice causes more pain to animals than it gives pleasure to man; is that practice moral or immoral? And if, exactly in proportion as human beings raise their heads out of the slough of selfishness, they do not with one voice answer "Immoral," let the morality of the principle of utility be forever condemned.

MONTAIGNE, MICHEL DE *(1533-1592, French essayist)*

For my part I have never been able to see, without displeasure, an innocent and defenseless animal, from whom we receive no offense or harm, pursued and slaughtered.

* * *

Plato, in his picture of the golden age under Saturn, reckons, among the chief advantages that a man then had, his communication with beasts, of whom, inquiring and informing himself, he knew the true qualities and differences of them all, by which he acquired a very perfect intelligence and prudence, and led his life more happily than we could do. Need we a better proof to condemn human imprudence in the concern of beasts?

(from "An Apology of Raymond Sebond")

OVID *(43 B.C.-17? A.D.; Roman poet)*

Forbear, O mortals,
To spoil your bodies with such impious food!
There is corn for you, apples, whose weight bears down
The bending branches; there are grapes that swell
On the green vines, and pleasant herbs, and greens
Made mellow and soft with cooking; there is milk
And clover-honey. Earth is generous
With her provision, and her sustenance
Is very kind; she offers, for your tables,
Food that requires no bloodshed and no slaughter.

* * *

Oh, Ox, how great are thy desserts! A being without guile, harmless, simple, willing for work! Ungrateful and unworthy of the fruits of earth, man his own farm laborer slays and smites with the axe that toil-worn neck that had so oft renewed for him the face of the hard earth; so many harvests given!

* * *

Alas, what wickedness to swallow flesh into our own flesh, to fatten our greedy bodies by cramming in other bodies, to have one living creature fed by the death of another!

PLUTARCH (46?-120? A.D.; Greek biographer and historian, most famous for his Lives)

I for my part do much marvel at what sort of feeling, soul or reason the first man with his mouth touched slaughter, and reached to his lips the flesh of a dead animal, and having set before people courses of ghastly corpses and ghosts, could give those parts the names of meat and victuals that but a little before lowed, cried, moved, and saw; how his sight could endure the blood of the slaughtered, flayed, and mangled bodies; how his smell could bear their scent; and how the very nastiness happened not to offend the taste while it chewed the sores of others, and participated of the sap and juices of deadly wounds.

* * *

But whence is it that a certain ravenousness and frenzy drives you in these happy days to pollute yourselves with blood, since you have such an abundance of things necessary for your subsistence? Why do you belie the earth as unable to maintain you?... Are you not ashamed to mix tame fruits with blood and slaughter? You are indeed wont to call serpents, leopards, and lions savage creatures; but yet yourselves are defiled with blood, and come nothing behind them in cruelty. What they kill is their ordinary nourishment, but what you kill is your better fare.

* * *

For we eat not lions and wolves by way of revenge, but we let those go and catch the harmless and tame sort, such as have neither stings nor teeth to bite with, and slay them.

* * *

But if you will contend that yourself were born to an inclination to such food as you have now a mind to eat, do you then yourself kill what you would eat. But do it yourself, without the help of a chopping-knife, mallet, or axe—as wolves, bears, and lions do, who kill and eat at once. Rend an ox with thy teeth, worry a hog with thy mouth, tear a lamb or a hare in pieces, and fall on and eat it alive as they do. But if thou hadst rather stay until what thou eatest is to become dead, and if thou art loath to force a soul out of its body, why then dost thou against Nature eat an animate thing?

(from *Of Eating of Flesh*)

POPE, ALEXANDER *(1688-1744, English poet)*

> But just disease to luxury succeeds,
> And every death its own avenger breeds;
> The fury passions from that blood began,
> And turn'd on man a fiercer savage—Man.

(from *Essay on Man*)

PORPHYRY *(232-?A.D.; Greek philosopher, author of a number of philosophical treatises)*

He who abstains from anything animate...will be much more careful not to injure those of his own species. For he who loves the genus will not hate any species of animals.

* * *

But to deliver animals to be slaughtered and cooked, and thus be filled with murder, not for the sake of nutriment and satisfying the wants of nature, but making pleasure and gluttony the end of such conduct, is transcendently iniquitous and dire.

* * *

And is it not absurd, since we see that many of our own species live from sense alone, but do not possess intellect and reason; and since we also see that many of them surpass the most terrible of wild beasts in cruelty, anger, and rapine, being murderous of their children and their parents, and also being tyrants and the tools of kings [it is not, I say absurd] to fancy that we ought to act justly towards these, but that no justice is due from us to the ox that ploughs, the dog that is fed with us, and the animals that nourish us with their milk and adorn our bodies with their wool? Is not such an opinion most irrational and absurd?

(from *On Abstinence from Animal Food*)

PRASAD, DR. RAJENDRA *(1884-1963, first President of the Republic of India)*

Any integrated view of life as a whole will reveal to us the connection between the individual's food and his behavior towards others, and through a process of ratiocination which is not fantastic, we cannot but arrive at the conclusion that the only means of escaping the hydrogen bomb is to escape the [type of] mentality which has produced it, and the only way to escape that mentality is to cultivate respect for all life, life in all forms, under all conditions. It is only another name for vegetarianism.

PYTHAGORAS *(578?-510? B.C.; Greek philosopher and mathematician; called founder of European science and philosophy)*

If men with fleshly mortals must be fed,
And chaw with bleeding teeth the breathing bread;
What else is this but to devour our guests,
And barbarously renew Cyclopean feasts?
While Earth not only can your needs supply,
But, lavish of her store, provides for luxury;
A guiltless feast administers with ease,
And without blood is prodigal to please.

SALT, HENRY S. *(1851-1939, English humanitarian and reformer, friend of Gandhi and Shaw)*

On the contrary, I suggest that in proportion as man is truly "humanised," not by schools of cookery but by schools of thought, he will abandon the barbarous habit of his flesh-eating ancestors, and will make gradual progress towards a purer, simpler, more humane, and therefore more civilised diet-system.

* * *

The cattle-ships of the present day reproduce, in an aggravated form, some of the worst horrors of the slave-ships of fifty years back. . . . The present system of killing animals for food is a very cruel and barbarous one, and a direct outrage on what I have termed the "humanities of diet."

* * *

You take a beautiful girl down to supper and you offer her—a ham sandwich! It is proverbial folly to cast pearls before swine. What are we to say of the politeness which casts swine before pearls?

* * *

Vegetarianism is the diet of the future, as flesh-food is the diet of the past. In that striking and common contrast, a fruit shop side by side with a butcher's, we have a most significant object lesson. There, on the one hand, are the barbarities of a savage custom—the headless carcasses, stiffened into a ghastly semblance of life, the joints and steaks and gobbets with their sickening odour, the harsh grating of the bone-saw, and the dull thud of the chopper—a perpetual crying protest against the horrors of flesh-eating. And as if this were not witness sufficient, here close alongside is a wealth of golden fruit, a sight to make a poet happy, the only food that is entirely congenial to the physical structure and the natural instincts of mankind, that can entirely satisfy the highest human aspirations. Can we doubt, as we gaze at this contrast, that whatever intermediate steps may need to be gradually taken, whatever difficulties to be overcome, the path of progression from the barbarities to the humanities of diet lies clear and unmistakable before us?

* * *

This logic of the larder is the very negation of a true reverence for life, for it implies that the real lover of animals is he whose larder is fullest of them:

He prayeth best, who eateth best
All things both great and small.

It is the philosophy of the wolf, the shark, the cannibal.

(from *The Humanities of Diet*)

SCHOPENHAUER, ARTHUR *(1788-1860, German philosopher)*

Since compassion for animals is so intimately associated with goodness of character, it may be confidently asserted that whoever is cruel to animals cannot be a good man.

SCHWEITZER, ALBERT *(1875-1965, renowned medical missionary in Africa, theologian, and musician; winner of Nobel Peace Prize of 1952)*

Wherever any animal is forced into the service of man the sufferings which it has to bear on that account are the concern of every one of us. No one ought to permit, in so far as he can prevent it, pain or suffering for which he will not take the responsibility. No one ought to rest at ease in the thought that in so doing he would mix himself up in affairs which are not his business. Let no one shirk the burden of his responsibility. When there is so much maltreatment of animals, when the cries of thirsting creatures go up unnoticed from the railway trucks, when there is so much roughness in our slaughterhouses, when in our kitchens so many animals suffer horrible deaths from unskillful hands, when animals endure unheard-of agonies from heartless men, or are delivered to the dreadful play of children, then we are all guilty and must bear the blame.

* * *

It is *good* to maintain and cherish life; it is *evil* to destroy and to check life.

* * *

A man is really ethical only when he obeys the constraint laid on him to help all life which he is able to succour, and when he goes out of his way to avoid injuring anything living. He does not ask how far this or that life deserves sympathy as valuable in itself, nor how far it is capable of feeling. To him life as such is sacred. He shatters no ice crystal that sparkles in the sun, tears no leaf from its tree, breaks off no flower, and is careful not to crush any insect as he walks. If he works by lamplight on a summer evening, he prefers to keep the window shut and to breathe stifling air rather than to see insect after insect fall on his table with singed and sinking wings.

* * *

The very fact that the animal, as a victim of research, has in his pain rendered such services to suffering men has itself created a new and unique relation of solidarity between him and ourselves. The result is that a fresh obligation is laid on each of us to do as much good as we possibly can to all creatures in all sorts of circumstances. When I help an insect out of his troubles all that I do is to attempt to remove some of the guilt contracted through these crimes against animals.

SENECA *(4? B.C.-65 A.D.; Roman philosopher, dramatist and statesman)*

If true, the Pythagorean principles as to abstaining from flesh foster innocence; if ill-founded they at least teach us frugality, and what loss have you in losing your cruelty? I merely deprive you of the food of lions and vultures. We shall recover our sound reason only if we shall separate ourselves from the herd—the very fact of the approbation of the multitude is a proof of the unsoundness of the opinion or practice. Let us ask what is best, not what is customary. Let us love temperance—let us be just—let us refrain from bloodshed.

SHAW, GEORGE BERNARD *(1856-1950, British dramatist and critic)*

Why should you call me to account for eating decently? If I battened on the scorched corpses of animals, you might well ask me why I did that.

* * *

When a man wants to murder a tiger, he calls it sport; when a tiger wants to murder him he calls it ferocity.

* * *

Animals are my friends...and I don't eat my friends.

* * *

My will contains directions for my funeral, which will be followed not by mourning coaches, but by herds of oxen, sheep, swine, flocks of poultry, and a small traveling aquarium of live fish, all wearing white scarves in honor of the man who perished rather than eat his fellow creatures.

* * *

We are the living graves of murdered beasts,
Slaughtered to satisfy our appetites.
We never pause to wonder at our feasts,
If animals, like men, can possibly have rights.
We pray on Sundays that we may have light,
To guide our foot-steps on the paths we tread.
We're sick of war, we do not want to fight,
The thought of it now fills our hearts with dread
And yet we gorge ourselves upon the dead.
Like carrion crows, we live and feed on meat,
Regardless of the suffering and pain
We cause by doing so. If thus we treat
Defenceless animals for sport or gain,
How can we hope in this world to attain
The Peace we say we are so anxious for?
We pray for it, o'er hecatombs of slain,
To God, while outraging the moral law,
Thus cruelty begets its offspring—War.

Song of Peace

SHELLEY, PERCY BYSSHE *(1792-1822, English poet)*

It is only by softening and disguising dead flesh by culinary preparation that it is rendered susceptible of mastication or digestion, and that the sight of its bloody juices and red horror does not excite intolerable loathing and disgust. Let the advocate of animal food force himself to a decisive experiment on its fitness, and as Plutarch recommends, tear a living lamb with his teeth and, plunging his head into its vitals, slake his thirst with the steaming blood; when fresh from the deed of horror let him revert to the irresistible instincts of nature that would rise in judgment against it, and say, "Nature formed me for such work as this." Then, and then only, would he be consistent.

SHELTON, DR. HERBERT *(1895-, American naturopathic physician)*

The cannibal goes out and hunts, pursues and kills another man and proceeds to cook and eat him precisely as he would any other game. There is not a single argument nor a single fact that can be offered in favor of flesh eating that cannot be offered, with equal strength, in favor of cannibalism.

(from *Superior Nutrition*)

SINGER, ISAAC BASHEVIS *(1904-, writer, Nobel Laureate)*

. . . Verily, in order to create the world, the Infinite One had had to shrink His light; there could be no free choice without pain. But since the beasts were not endowed with free choice, why should they have to suffer?

(from *The Slaughter*)

TAGORE, RABINDRANATH *(1861-1941, Nobel Prize winning Hindu poet)*

We manage to swallow flesh only because we do not think of the cruel and sinful thing we do. There are many crimes which are the creation of man himself, the wrongfulness of which is put down to his divergence from habit, custom, or tradition. But cruelty is not of these. It is a fundamental sin, and admits of no arguments or nice distinctions. If only we do not allow our heart to grow callous it protects against cruelty, is always clearly heard; and yet we go on perpetrating cruelties easily, merrily, all of us—in fact, any one who does not join in is dubbed a crank. . . . If, after our pity is aroused, we persist in throttling our feelings simply in order to join others in preying upon life, we insult all that is good in us. I have decided to try a vegetarian diet.

THOREAU, HENRY DAVID *(1817-1862, U.S. naturalist and writer)*

I have no doubt that it is part of the destiny of the human race in its gradual development to leave off the eating of animals as surely as the savage tribes have left off eating each other when they came into contact with the more civilized.

TOLSTOY, LEO (1828-1920, Russian novelist and social theorist)

Vegetarianism serves as a criterion by which we know that the pursuit of moral perfection on the part of man is genuine and sincere.

* * *

This is dreadful! Not the suffering and death of the animals, but that man suppresses in himself, unnecessarily, the highest spiritual capacity—that of sympathy and pity towards living creatures like himself—and by violating his own feelings becomes cruel. And how deeply seated in the human heart is the injunction not to take life!

VOLTAIRE, FRANCOIS *(1694-1778, French writer and philosopher)*

[Porphyry] regards other animals as our brothers, because they are endowed with life as we are, because they have the same principles of life, the same feelings, the same ideas, memory, industry—as we. [Human] speech alone is wanting to them. If they had it should we dare to kill and eat them? Should we dare to commit these fratricides?

(from *Viande*)

WELLS, H.G. *(1866-1946, English novelist and historian)*

In all the round world of Utopia there is no meat. There used to be. But now we cannot stand the thought of slaugterhouses. And in a population that is all educated and at about the same level of physical refinement, it is practically impossible to find anyone who will hew a dead ox or pig. We never settled the hygienic aspect of meat-eating at all. This other aspect decided us. I can still remember as a boy the rejoicings over the closing of the last slaughterhouse.

(from *A Modern Utopia*)

WILCOX, ELLA WHEELER *(1853[?]-1919, American poet and novelist)*

I am the voice of the voiceless.
Through me the dumb shall speak
Til' the deaf world's ear shall be made to hear
The wrongs of the wordless weak.
The same force formed the sparrow
That fashioned man, the king.
The God of the whole gave a spark of soul
To furred and feathered thing;
And I am my brother's keeper,
And I will fight his fight.
And speak the word for beast and bird
Till the world shall set things right

FAMOUS VEGETARIANS

Alcott, Louisa May
Aristotle
Barton, Clara
Besant, Annie
Buddha
Cicero
Darwin, Charles
Diogenes
Einstein, Albert
Epicurus
Franklin, Benjamin
Gandhi, Mohandas
Graham, Sylvester
Greeley, Horace
Herodotus
Horace
Kellogg, John Harvey
Montaigne, Michel de
Montgomery, Field Marshal Lord
More, Sir Thomas
Newton, Sir Isaac
Ovid

Plato
Plutarch
Pope, Alexander
Porphyry
Pythagoras
Rousseau, Jean Jacques
Seneca
Shakespeare
Shaw, George Bernard
Shelley, Percy and Mary
Sinclair, Upton
Socrates
Swedenborg, Emanuel
Tagore, Rabindranath
Tolstoy, Leo
Virgil
Voltaire, Francois
Wagner, Richard
Wells, H.G.
Wesley, John
Wilcox, Ella Wheeler

5/FURTHER READING

Animal Liberation, by Peter Singer (New York: New York Review, 1975; paperback: New York: Avon, 1975).

> One of the best, if not the best, all-round book on animal welfare. Singer, a professor of philosophy, discusses the ethics and morality governing our relation with animals, documents the cruelties to animals raised for slaughter and experimentation, shows how to become a vegetarian, and even includes vegetarian recipes in his authoritative book.

Animal Rights and Human Obligations, Tom Regan and Peter Singer, eds. (Englewood Cliffs, N.J.: Prentice Hall, 1976).

> A series of essays by well-known philosophers and humanitarians of the past and present, arguing the pros and cons, but mostly pros, of the subject, Do animals have rights? and Do humans have obligations toward them?

On Abstinence From Animal Food, Porphyry, trans. from the Greek by Thomas Taylor, ed. Esme Wynne-Tyson (London: Centaur; Boston: Brandon, 1965)

> A third-century philosopher, Porphyry was rated by many of his contemporaries as wiser and more erudite than Plato. This book shows how keenly he and other ancient Greek "pagans" observed and understood the mind of animals, and how tellingly he and they exposed the specious arguments seeking to justify animal sacrifice and slaughter.

Animals, Men and Morals: An Enquiry Into the Maltreatment of Non-humans, eds. Stanley and Roslind Godlovitch and John Harris (London: Gollancz; New York; Taplinger, 1972).

Thirteen essays by contributors who write with conviction and authority about animal abuse and exploitation from the perspectives of ethics, ecology, and sociology.

Animal Machines, Ruth Harrison (London: Stuart, 1964).
One of the first books to describe factory farming and its effect on animals.

Eating for Life, Nathaniel Altman (Wheaton, Ill.: Theosophical Pub. House, 1973).
A well-documented easy-to-read book on vegetarianism, mostly concerned with the health and nutritional aspects of a fleshless diet but also touching upon the morality and ethics of animal slaughter.

Animal Rights, Patricia Curtis (New York: Four Winds, 1980).
A sobering look at the ways in which we exploit animals, by a journalist and animal welfare activist.

Man Kind? Our Incredible War on Wildlife, Cleveland Amory (New York: Harper and Row, 1974; paperback: New York: Dell, 1975).
The story of the aggressive and courageous efforts of one man, the president of The Fund for Animals, to preserve our wildlife from the savage attacks of that super-predator, man.

Cooking and Nutrition

Diet for a Small Planet, Frances Moore Lappé (New York: Ballantine, 1971).
Protein, protein, protein—how to get more and more of it in the right combinations from a meatless diet; with numerous recipes.

Laurel's Kitchen: A Handbook for Vegetarian Cookery and Nutrition, Laurel Robertson, Carol Flinders, and Bronwen Godfrey (Petaluma, Calif.: Nilgiri, 1976; paperback: New York: Bantam, 1978).

Excellent vegetarian recipes as well as abundant information on nutrition.

The Vegetarian Epicure, Anna Thomas (New York: Knopf, 1972; paperback, New York: Vintage, 1972).
   Gourmet vegetarian recipes, with the emphasis on taste.

Ten Talents, Dr. and Mrs. Frank Hurd (pub. by the authors, Chisholm, Minn.; available through the Seventh Day Adventist Church).
   An especially helpful book for those whose diet does not include dairy products or eggs (as well as meat of course).

Cook With Tofu, Christina Clarke (New York & Toronto: Avon/Madison Press Books, 1981).
   Long-tested tofu (soya bean curd) recipes adapted to Western tastes by cooks of the Rochester Zen Center, the author, and individuals and restaurants throughout the U.S. and Canada.

NOTES AND GLOSSARY

1. Lillie Wilson, "Animal Rights: A Return to Responsibility," *New Age*, Feb. 1981, p. 53.
2. *Pali:* the language in which the scriptures of Theravada Buddhism are written. Also known as Southern Buddhism, the Theravada arose in India and traveled from there to Sri Lanka, Burma, Thailand, Cambodia, and to Vietnam, Laos, and the West.
3. *Mahayana:* lit., "large vehicle," i.e., the Northern branch of the Buddha's teachings, which arose in northern India and spread to Mongolia, Sikkim, Bhutan, Nepal, China, Japan, Korea, Europe, and North America.
4. David Nevin, "Scientist Helps Stir New Movement for 'Animal Rights,'" *Smithsonian*, Apr. 1980, p. 56.
5. Peter Singer, *Animal Liberation* (New York: New York Review; paperback: Avon, 1975), p. 144.
6. Upton Sinclair, *The Jungle* (New York: New American Lib., 1905), pp. 39-40.
7. Richard Rhodes, "Watching the Animals," *Harper's*, March 1970.
8. Rev. Roy B. Oliver, "Why I Am a Vegetarian," *National Insider*, Oct. 3, 1975.
9. Singer, pp. 160-61.
10. Singer, pp. 162-63.
11. Singer, p. 175.
12. "Vegetarianism: Can You Get By Without Meat?" *Consumer Reports*, June 1980, pp. 357-65.
13. See literature of the organization Animal Liberation (not to be confused with the book by the same name), from which this has been adapted.
14. *Shakyamuni:* lit., "sage of the Shakya clan," one of the appellations of the Buddha, whose own name was Siddhartha Gautama.
15. The other nine precepts are: 2) not to take what is not given, 3) not to engage in improper sexuality, 4) not to lie, 5) not to cause others to use liquors or drugs that confuse or weaken the mind nor to do so

oneself, 6) not to speak of the shortcomings of others, 7) not to praise oneself and condemn others, 8) not to withhold material or spiritual aid, 9) not to become angry, and 10) not to revile the three treasures of Buddha, Dharma, and Sangha (those who follow the Buddha's Dharma, or teaching).

16. Buddha-nature: state in which everything is subject to endless transformation; that which is dynamic, devoid of shape, color, and mass; the matrix of all phenomena.

17. Hakuun Yasutani, *Reflections on the Five Ranks, the Three Resolutions, and the Ten Precepts*, 1962, trans. Kenneth Kraft.

18. *Buddha:* a Sanskrit word used in two senses: 1) ultimate truth or absolute mind, and 2) one awakened or enlightened to the true nature of existence.

19. *Dialogues of the Buddha*, Vol. III of *Sacred Books of the Buddhists*, ed. T.W. Rhys Davids (London: Oxford Univ. Press, 1910), p. 137.

20. *Madly Singing in the Mountains: An Appreciation and Anthology of Arthur Waley*, ed. Ivan Morris, p. 342.

21. Edward Thomas, *The Life of Buddha* (London: Routledge, 1949), p. 149.

22. Mrs. Rhys Davids, *A Manual of Buddhism* (London: Sheldon, 1932), p. 260.

23. *Dharma:* a Buddhist term meaning "ultimate truth," "the law of the universe," or "the Buddha's teaching."

24. *roshi:* lit., "venerable teacher."

25. The *Mahavagga* [*Vinaya Texts* (Part II), Vol. XVII of *Sacred Books of the East*, ed. F. Max Muller (London: Oxford Univ. Press, 1882), p. 88] records such an incident, in which a certain Brahmana approaches Ananda to ask:

> "If I were to prepare, my dear Ananda, rice-milk and honey-lumps (for the Bhikkhus), would the reverend Gotama accept it from me?"
>
> "Well, my good Brahmana, I will ask the Blessed One." And the venerable Ananda told this thing to the Blessed One.
>
> "Well, Ananda, let him prepare (those dishes)."
>
> "Well, my good Brahmana, you may prepare (those dishes)."

26. *sushi:* vinegared rice cakes topped with raw fish or wrapped in seaweed.

27. This was neither Harada-roshi nor Yasutani-roshi.

28. *karma:* one of the fundamental doctrines of Buddhism, karma means action and reaction, or the law of causation on a personal level. Our present life and circumstances are the product of our past thoughts and actions, and in the same way our deeds in this life will fashion our future mode of existence.

29. According to Theravada sources, the Buddha did drink milk but only from a cow whose calf was at least ten days old.
30. *Majjhima Nikaya*, trans. Lord Chalmers.
31. I.B. Horner, *Early Buddhism and the Taking of Life* (Kandy: Buddhist Publication Soc., 1967).
32. According to Hindu teachings, food is of three kinds: *sattvic, rajasic,* and *tamasic.* Sattvic, or pure food, is food that induces a tranquil state. This includes fruits, nuts, milk products, vegetables, grains, beans, and cereals. When the same foods are mixed with a lot of spices they become rajasic, that is, they create restlessness in body and mind. Rajasic food also includes every kind of animal flesh. Foods that are old or overripe or that have been cooked and kept for a long time lose their sattvic quality and become tamasic.
33. Henry S. Salt, "The Humanities of Diet," in *Animal Rights and Human Obligations*, eds. Tom Regan and Peter Singer (Englewood Cliffs, N.J.: Prentice-Hall, 1976), pp. 143-44.
34. Esme Wynne-Tyson, ed., *On Abstinence from Animal Food*, by Porphyry, trans. Thomas Taylor (London: Centaur, 1965; Boston: Brandon), p. 8.
35. For a detailed explanation of this rule, see *A Record of the Buddhist Religion*, I. Tsing, trans. J. Takakusu (Delhi: Munshriram Manoharlal, 1966), pp. 30-33.
36. *The Lankavatara Sutra*, trans. Daisetz Suzuki (London: Routledge, 1932).
37. *Dyana:* "concentration of mind," a one-pointed, concentrated and awakened mind.
38. *Samadhi:* equilibrium, tranquility, and one-pointedness, a state of intense yet effortless concentration, of complete absorption of the mind in itself, of heightened and expanded awareness.
39. *Parinirvana:* lit., "complete extinction," a term usually referring to the passing away of the Buddha.
40. *Kalpa:* the period of time between the beginning of a world cycle and its extinction; an incalculably long time.
41. *A Buddhist Bible*, ed. Dwight Goddard (New York: Dutton, 1952), pp. 264-65.
42. *Encyclopedia of Buddhism*, ed. G.P. Malalasekera (Govt. of Ceylon Press, 1963), I, 2, 291.
43. Robert Ozaki, *The Japanese* (Tokyo: Tuttle, 1978), p. 99.
44. Eihei Dogen, "Hokyo-ki: Zen Master, Zen Disciple," trans. Wako Kato and Daizen Victoria, in *Udumbara, A Journal of Zen Master Dogen*, I (1980), 2.
45. Holmes Welch, *The Practice of Chinese Buddhism, 1900-1950* (Boston: Harvard Univ. Press, 1967), p. 112.
46. *Tantric:* esoteric or mystical teachings.

47. Alexandra David-Neel, *Buddhism: Its Doctrines and Its Methods* (New York: Avon, 1977), p. 161.
48. *Vedas:* ancient sacred books of Hinduism, consisting of psalms, chants, sacred writing, etc.
49. Upanishads: a group of late Vedic metaphysical treatises dealing with man in relation to the universe.
50. Koshelya Walli, *The Conception of Ahimsa in Indian Thought* (Varanasi, India: Battacharya, 1974).
51. Mircea Eliade, *From Primitives to Zen* (San Francisco: Harper and Row, 1967), p. 176.
52. "The Seventh Pillar Edict," in *Sources of Indian Tradition*, trans. Wm. de Barry et al. (New York: Columbia Univ. Press, 1958).
53. *A Record of Buddhistic Kingdoms*, trans. James Legge (New York: Dover, 1965), p. 43.
54. *Dialogues of the Buddha*, p. 255.
55. A. Foucher, *The Life of the Buddha* (Middletown, Conn.: Wesleyan Univ. Press, 1963), p. 183.
56. Edward Conze, *Thirty Years of Buddhist Studies* (Columbia, S.C.: Univ. of S.C. Press, 1968).
57. Mrs. Rhys Davids, *A Manual of Buddhism.*
58. *Bodhisattva:* lit., "wisdom being"; anyone who, having attained enlightenment, dedicates himself to helping others do the same.
59. Reprinted in *The Denver Post*, Nov. 30, 1979.
60. Divers who have approached swimming whales at close range claim that they do indeed utter cries of distress. The renowned Jacques Cousteau reported the testimony of two of his divers who on July 22, 1980, came upon a whale entangled in a heavy net: "Confused, exhausted, it cried in plaintive moans to migrating companions now perhaps far away." (The divers, by patiently petting the whale until it had become calm, were able to free it.)
61. Daisetz T. Suzuki, *The Chain of Compassion* (Cambridge, Mass.: Cambridge Buddhist Assoc., 1966), pp. 12-13.
62. Donna Barnett, *The Whig-Standard* (Kingston, Ontario), July 29, 1980.
63. Dr. Hugh Drummond, *Mother Jones*, Feb/Mar 1977.
64. It has been shown through laboratory analysis that the oil of the jojoba, a common desert shrub, is nearly identical to sperm whale oil, with the same wide range of industrial and other uses. "Jojoba can do everything the animal oil does—and more" (*Science Digest*, Aug. 1980).
65. Victor B. Scheffer, *The Year of the Whale* (New York: Scribner, 1969), p. 167.
66. Lewis Regenstein, "Will Congress Save the Dolphins?" *Defenders of Wildlife News*, Jan.-Feb. 1972, p. 30.

67. Geoffrey Grigson, *The Goddess of Love* (Briarcliff: Stein, 1976), p. 137.
68. Konrad Lorenz, *Man Meets Dog* (New York: Penguin, 1953), pp. vii, ix.
69. Eliade, p. 173.
70. W.S. Collin and R.B. Dobbin, *Circulation* (Supplement 2), Vol. 31-32, as quoted in "Do Human Beings Need Meat?" Mervyn G. Hardinge, *Review and Herald*, Feb. 27, 1969.
71. Hitler's avoidance of meat for health reasons may have been his most level-headed policy. See Supplement 2.
72. Patrick Corbett, *Animals, Men, and Morals*, eds. Stanley and Roslind Godlovitch and John Harris (New York: Taplinger, 1972), p. 233.

SUPPLEMENTS

1. Carl C. Pfeiffer, *Mental and Elemental Nutrients* (New Canaan: Keats, 1975), p. 102.
2. H.C. Sherman, "Protein Requirement of Maintenance in Man and the Nutritive Efficiency of Bread Protein," *Journal of Biological Chemistry*, 41 (1920), 97.
3. Mervyn G. Hardinge and Frederick J. Stare, "Nutritional Studies of Vegetarians," *Journal of Clinical Nutrition*, 2 (1954), 76.
4. L. Jean Bogert et al., *Nutrition and Physical Fitness*, 8th ed. (1966), pp. 106-7.
5. Nathaniel Altman, *Eating for Life* (Wheaton, Ill.: Theosophical Pub. House, 1973), pp. 22-23.
6. Altman, pp. 23-24.
7. Pfeiffer, p. 105. Also, Sir Stanley Davidson and R. Passmore, *Human Nutrition and Dietetics*, 1963 ed., p. 81.
8. R. Bressani and M. Behar, "The Use of Plant Protein Foods in Preventing Malnutrition," in E.S. Livingston, ed.: *Proceedings of the Sixth International Congress of Nutrition* (Edinburgh, 1964), p. 182.
9. C.A. Keele and E. Neil, *Sampson Wright's Applied Physiology* (11th ed. rev., 1965), p. 418.
10. G. Yukawa, "The Absolute Vegetarian Diet of Japanese Bonzes," *Arch. f. Verdauungskr.*, Berlin 15 (1909), 471.
11. *The Lancet*, 43 (1963), 285.
12. *Journal of the American Dietetic Assoc.*, 62 (1973), 257.
13. Rudolph M. Ballantine, Jr., "Transition to Vegetarianism," *Himalayan News*, Jan. 1978.
14. Mervyn G. Hardinge et al., "Nutritional Studies of Vegetarians (V)," *Journal of the Amer. Dietetic Assoc.*, 48 (1966), 27.
15. Editorial, *The Lancet* (London), 2 (1959), 956.

16. Paavo Airola, *How to Get Well* (Phoenix: Health Plus, 1974), p. 194.
17. Bandaru Reddy and Ernest Wynder, *Journal of the National Cancer Institute*, 50: 1437-1442, 1973.
18. "Diet and Stress in Vascular Disease," *Journal of the American Medical Association*, Vol. 176, No. 9, June 3, 1961, p. 806.
19. *The Encyclopaedia Brittanica*, 1967 ed., Vol. 22, p. 935.
20. Mimi Sheraton, "What *Is* Safe to Eat?" Rochester, N.Y. *Times-Union*, June 11, 1980.
21. Frances Moore Lappé, *Diet for a Small Planet* (New York: Ballantine, 1971), p. 19.
22. *Facts of Vegetarianism*, p. 8.
23. Don Kendall, Rochester, N.Y. *Democrat and Chronicle*, Apr. 6, 1980.
24. Stephen Singular, "Saving People from Wonder Drugs," *Quest*, May 1980.
25. Albert Levy, *The Meat Handbook* (Westport, Conn.: Avi, 1967), p. 13.
26. Dale Shurter and Eugene Walter, "The Meat You Eat," *The Plain Truth*, Oct-Nov. 1970.
27. Altman, p. 36.
28. *Ahimsa*, Sept. 1962, as reported in *Facts of Vegetarianism*, p. 8.
29. *The New York Times*, March 4, 1968, p. 74.
30. William Robbins, "Meat-Poultry Plant Check Finds 38 of 88 Are Dirty," *The New York Times*, June 18, 1973, p. 1.
31. Donald Patton, *The United States and World Resources* (New Jersey: Van Nostrand, 1968), p. 112.
32. "The World Food Problem," a report by the President's Science Advisory Committee, Vol. II, May 1967.
33. Lappé, p. 13.
34. A.H. Boerma, *Food Requirements and Production Possibilities*, United Nations Economic and Social Council (UNESCO), Paris, p. 12.
35. Frances Moore Lappé and Joseph Collins, *Food First* (New York: Ballantine, 1977), p. 238.
36. Frances Moore Lappé and Joseph Collins, *World Hunger: Ten Myths*, rev. ed. (Berkeley: Institute for Food and Development Policy, 1978), p. 8.
37. Lappé and Collins, *World Hunger*, p. 19.
38. Lappé and Collins, *Food First*, p. 47.
39. Aaron M. Altschul, *Proteins: Their Chemistry and Politics* (New York: Basic Books, 1965), p. 265.
40. Ron Litton, *Terracide*.
41. *Georg Borgstrom, The Food and People Dilemma* (Duxbury, 1973), p. 103.